MW00422803

Everyday Spirits

Everyday Spirits

David Appelbaum

State University of New York Press

Published by
State University of New York Press, Albany

© 1993   State University of New York

For information, address State University of New York
Press, State University Plaza, Albany, NY 12246

Production by Dana Foote
Marketing by Dana E. Yanulavich

Library of Congress Cataloging-in-Publication Data

Appelbaum David.
    Everyday spirits / David Appelbaum.
        p.   cm.
    ISBN 0-7914-1583-X (alk. paper). : ISBN 0-7914-1584-8 (pbk. :
alk. paper)
    1. Self (Philosophy). 2. Home—Philosophy. 3. Sense (Philosophy)
I. Title.
BD438.5.A66   1993
191—dc20   92-32009
                                                      CIP

10 9 8 7 6 5 4 3 2 1

Grasp and use, but never name.
—Rinzai Gigen

CONTENTS

PREFACE

This book is a home for me. It was written because I live in a home. For almost all of my life, I have lived in a home. My experiences predominantly are of articles of home dwelling—teacups, brooms, pillow slips, the oven, door hinges, picture hooks, and lamps. Now that I keep a house, I am a householder.

Yet I also seek a way to become whole. As I understand it, the search involves a leaves-taking and journey. One bids farewell to one's former life and, faring forth, welcomes a new one. It is both process and event. Given my station, the commitment has always come with a question. Is there a way to wholeness through my place of dwelling, my house?

It is important, I feel, to guard against a literal-minded interpretation of journeying. Fairy tales repeatedly tell of a sojourn in which hero or heroine never leaves home, never ventures forth in the world. But where or what in the house gives access to a view of a new land? I gradually have come to acknowledge it has to do with the viewer, myself.

Moving about the house, I am not always the same. Most often, I am perceiver of the tried, true, and tested. More rarely, of an unaccustomed freshness, a novel vista, an open doorway. Moments in which another level of reality appears provide an enigmatic clue. A chipped teapot, invisibly dispensable most of the time, suddenly becomes an object of inestimable value. What mysterious transaction brings about a change? Rilke first pointed me toward an answer. A householder uniquely is able to speak of our world from the standpoint of *dwelling*. Imagine (Rilke suggests) talking with an angel, a being of the higher world. What would rivet his attention? What, from his superior vantage point, would be unknown? "Tell him of Things. He will stand astonished" (*Duino Elegies*). Conversely, through Things am I related to a world of which fairy tale and angel speak.

My home is where I house the Things of my life. An implicit relation with them in inexplicable moments becomes explicit, substantial, and transforming. Tools, implements, instruments, utensils, articles, furnishings, paraphernalia, bric-a-brac, and the other stuff of my house call me to astonishment—where the angel stands. Their call can open a way of seeing myself, of faring forth from an ordinary view to a panorama of extraordinary dimensions. When I respond, journeying is a matter of realigning energies within—not going without. To journey is to make my home available to a presence whose presence lends meaning to my life. To journey is to be hospitable.

My thoughts went out along these lines. I began to regard the things that lined my shelves and stood in corners, crannies, and cupboards, and in plain everyday view, with a questioning look. In honesty, I knew not what I saw and saw I did not know how to look. How, therefore, to tell?

One day, I found myself retrieving a walking stick that stood against a wall. It had been with me for years, an old friend, a hickory branch, dappled and gnarled, with a sort of steady and reliable character. It was a time of inner turmoil when a question burned in me. I did not know whether my house was a trap or a vehicle for spiritual discovery. The moment burst upon me. I had nothing to tell of the walking stick—or any other thing. I did not relate to it. I was not hospitable toward it. I had never listened to its story.

The recognition provided a germ for this book. This book is both promise and fruit of hospitality. The promise signified by listening to what each thing has to tell is consummated by its story showing forth. What astonishes me is how the story is no other than the thing itself. My telling of things has a home, and the home is this book. With each new telling (and retelling) in it, an understanding of the place I inhabit deepens. This I share. Not a blinding ray of light, but many shades faceted by nuance, detail, particularity, and difference appear with each step taken. It seems to me I offer nothing profound if not the profound beauty of a kitchen put back to order, a bedstead straightened, and the stairs well swept.

If (to return to my initial question) there is a way, an inner practice, for a householder, I say it concerns just such a walk about the home. See if houseplants need water, or front windows have been cleaned, or a lampshade gives the right tilt, or the pipes should be bled. Watch how it goes from day to day to day. This wears out a householder's shoe through the practice of keeping a home, and the way opens to a wider understanding. That is my hope here.

·

INTRODUCTION

A friend for whom philosophy performs the highest office—to guide the perplexed—once told a story. When still young, he was watching the countryside from a bus window. A mid-October morning filled the scene with magical changes of time and mood. The whole world was transformed by the first frost's work. Field and lawn had been blanched, stalks withered, and leaves dropped silently from their branches. The hour belonged to Jack Frost. One could almost feel his presence.

In one yard, children had etched a giant's circle by running their boots over the ground. They were in the midst of a game of fox and goose. The friend's companion let out a moan at the sight of it. "Look," she said, "the fox has the goose."

"No," his other companion disagreed, "the goose will get away."

As he listened to each side, the pessimist and the optimist, the scene took a different shape before his eyes. The path, a wheel outlined in frost with spokes through the hub, had a motion of its own. It spun around while the children were stationary on it. In fact, trees and houses, the road, the bus, the whole world, and the sky stood motionless in relation to the gyrating circle. His eyes would not leave it. Even after the bus moved on by, the image spread vividly in front of him for some time.

Meanwhile his companions continued their dispute. The truth had become a matter of honor. What did he think about the goose's capture? But his mind was elsewhere. The verdict on the goose belonged to the game. Both optimist and pessimist took the game literally. He had glimpsed another level, the game's animating force. This was as real a fact as the morning cold that stung the bare fingers. He had met the spirit of Jack Frost.

Such events are profoundly philosophical in the sense of Maimonides' great work, *The Guide for the Perplexed.* They mediate between the two realms of truth, the everyday and the extraordinary. They are balance wheel to the daily round, whose exaggerated claims would leave us bereft of memory of our duality. Their intrusion into our busy

xi

projects shocks and awakens us to a wider reality. The guidance of philosophy has much to do with alerting us to their existence and sensitizing us to their advent. Guidance in this sense returns us to the root meaning of the word. *To guide* is *to see, to know directly*, the Sanskrit *veda* comes from the same soil. We are guided by a vision of the whole—ourselves—and the greater whole—the Self.

A stick with two ends poses a challenge to mind: Which to grip? This is human perplexity. An easy singleness of choice, an empty monism, reflects an avoidance of thought. Of the two ways of blinding the eye to the twofoldness of humanity, overconcern with the ordinary is the modern one. All real difference is leveled and things are made objects, products, commodities, property, and possessions. In this Protagorean universe, being human is the measure of everything, and all is too, too human. A momentary opening to another reality—such as my friend's—is met with an explanatory denial. It is caused by suggestibility, poor education, or an aberration in physiology. Nothing more nor less. Empiricism thus makes us prisoners of the everyday condition, no longer free to grip the stick's other end.

The second escape route is no less dogmatic in its appeal. Dailiness distorts an absolute reality from which humans have been banished—"that man is stricken deaf and dumb and blind" (Yeats). As exiles who live only for their salvation, we revive in the moment of God's presence. A subtle sort of denial is practiced, what Nietzsche calls "inflation." The ordinary is rejected in favor of elevated experience. Tedium, *ennui*, and addiction, on the one side, together with fanatic moralism and intolerance, on the other, mark the plague. Its cost is the conspiratorial mind of the emigre. He or she walks the path of life dead to this world.

Our humanness has much to do with being guided by the moment. Spinoza notices that the receptive vision offers "the possibility of a much more powerful human nature." Its exercise, moreover, wholeheartedly embraces our dual origin and the contradictions it breeds. God and nature, heaven and earth, divine and mortal, absolute and relative, immutable and mutable: Being human, we need the ability to join these contrary aspects. But the two worlds—the chthonic and the celestial—are not contiguous. That they do not touch, as do lovers, but remain looking away from each other, indifferent enemies, is the source of all sorrow. The devilish gait of our nature ignores its higher purpose, while the angelic gaze disowns earthy desire. Our longing is for their mutual respect.

Plato is among the first to recognize the ineffectual contact of these aspects. He formulates the law of immiscibility. The law states that "the divine will not mingle directly with the human" (*Symposium* 203a). The perplexity that infects our condition stems from trying to mix the unmixable. The holy oil provided for anointing us does not go together with the waters of everyday life. That suffering is not relieved by application of any salve confirms the pessimist's position. The literal mind, moveover, draws further reason for its grim view. Aristotle founds a whole way of logical thinking on the law of the excluded middle. It says that a thing is either immortal or mortal but nothing in between. It thus transfers the unmixability of the two worlds to thought and establishes it there as supreme law.

Any cook's assistant knows better. Many of her tasks require the mixing of oil and water. She is asked to wash the dishes. If the plate is greasy, and grease does not rinse away with water, she tries a little soap. In the simple solution lies a profound matter. Whenever there are immiscible substances, there are emulsifiers. Their action consists of breaking down a refusal to intermingle while respecting the distinctness of partners. What occurs is no fusing or coupling, but rather a suspension of the will to remain apart. Emulsifiers are great coaxers, working with reticence or fear and bringing together substances proud of their separation. The result is a mixture of immiscibles. Our richest foods—milks, for example—come from the agreement to blend in this fashion.

Practical life abounds in counterexamples to the law of the excluded middle. The mind of nuance knows what a good host intuits—that the gathering's mix needs proper encouragement. Bald juxtaposition of guests may be ill-suited to their achieving friendship. An indirect approach must be sought. The matter of indirection cannot be one of force; a most violent agitation of salad dressing cannot prevent its eventual separation. Divorce cannot be undone by mandate. Instead, the help of a third party is enlisted. Marriage broker, peacemaker, mediator, go-between, the third finds a way to bring together the unreconciled sides. Its action is of intelligent obedience to the law of immiscibility—and to a higher law, of relation. That opposites attract is the law's simplest statement. That opposites need help in expressing their attraction is its corollary. The emulsifier is one of a class of helpers.

Thus soap is a method of guiding oil and water to a happy relation. Spinoza wonders about the soap for laving the divine together with the mortal. He finds method "in showing how the mind is to be guided to conform to the standard of already existing true knowledge." His discourse has great importance in a tradition for improving the understanding. The approach is the cook's assistant's: to clean the utensil and restore it to usefulness. The ordinary mind must be readied for knowledge of how to join separate parts of human nature. Perplexity lies in its being clogged and cluttered.

The approach is commendable, but what if one concentrated on the guides themselves—the third-party agents that gently (or not so gently) urge relation, the (so to speak) emulsifiers of inner life? Then one's philosophy would leave the mind to itself and dwell with the forces giving rise to the moment of ability.

Good philosophy may be pursued by compiling a census of guides. Rather than a text for elucidating method (how to soap), it then is a guidebook (to substances that work like soap.) It lists the guides, gives a brief description of each, and includes mention of special virtues or abilities. The guidebook is meant for travelers. Those who have left the familiar and ordinary in search of a much more powerful human nature may find themselves in foreign territory. Foreknowledge of how to conduct oneself and where to look for help may be invaluable. One may be able to obtain proper nourishment and live like a human being.

Danger lies waiting in such a guidebook, for compiler and reader alike. Agents that act as emulsifiers of the two fluids of humankind do not directly reveal themselves. Their indirect action is manifested as a gap or schism in the ordinary. One can speak of their presence best through a trace they leave—the dissolution of perplexity. My friend's experience is a case in point. The meeting with Jack Frost took place out of the corner of his eye, after noticing accoutrements and wraps. For the twinkling of an eye, his velocity and tempo matched Jack's. The result was an understanding of the whole that joined the parts. This was as clear as the trail blazed in morning frost.

The perishable part of us cannot keep the experience, and its residue falls upon the literal mind. Literal-mindedness lacks nuance and does not see a gap. Its confusion is our perplexity. Our credulity says one of two things: that the experience is unreal, like a fantasy, or that it is real, like a tree. The first is the pessimist who sees death in all events, the second the optimist who hopes the goose escapes.

To confuse the purpose of a guidebook is common. One may be bewitched into mistaking the description for the experience. This is a common error in many areas of human endeavor, and many professions find profit in it. Being forewarned, moreover, does not in itself dispel the illusion but may stem the need to act it out. When we see a stick bent in a glass of water, we do not try to straighten it. When we receive a moment of guidance, we do not straighten it to fit the book description.

The separateness of the two fundamental substances of human life further reveals the guides' qualifications and identities. Oil and water remain immiscible due to different solubilities. In us, heaven and earth fail to blend because of emotional, spatial, or temporal distance. Guidance is needed to cross the intermediate realm, and, in Plato's words, since guides are "between the two estates they weld both sides together and merge them into one great whole." They traverse the third world, ordinarily unknown to us, to bring back news of foreign lands. Functioning as messengers, they instruct and facilitate our movements throughout the middle ground. They open up passageways for us to follow—since it goes without saying that crossing is treacherous. Without a pilot, one gets lost in madness, illness, or death.

In all fairness, the guide is charged with duties besides the enlightenment of our lower nature. Its action upon us must prompt a reciprocal action upon the realm above ours. Plato's image of their "flying upward with our worship and our prayers" conveys the need of the higher for the denser, darker, and more gravid part of us. In joining the ordinary and the extraordinary, both are transformed. Heaven is thereby renewed, as a flower is by the bee that pollinates it. The law of immiscibility takes on a different light. It becomes a means of storing separate energies so that at a proper time their mixture may replenish the order of things.

The idea of a guidebook exposes a treachery in the language. About the guide, there is little agreement other than that the element belongs to experience. One removes it to express thought only like the thoughtful fisher, to return it to its medium. An angler learns more about himself than about his prize. In this way, although one does not avoid the illusion of knowing and owning the fish, one is less tempted to objectify it. Such fish exist only in water. Such guidance exists only in a moment when the two worlds achieve contact.

I have, moreover, taken a further risk in calling up an older term for the guide, the *daimon* or (in its Latinized version) *spirit*. Spirits, according to Plato, are neither mortal nor immortal, but, being "half-way between god and man," belong to the intermediate realm. They "ply between heaven and earth," cross-fertilizing the two worlds. What *spirits* in this sense denote has nothing to do with departed souls of the dead, apparitions, entities at mediumistic seances, ghosts, or other fictional or occult phenomena. Activity of spirits is remote from possession, demonry, the grotesque, the macabre, or other projections from the grotto of human consciousness. In a more rational vein, by *spirit* I do not mean the sentient part of a person or an individual's fate or destiny. Instead, spirits are agencies that join our human contradictories in a moment of union. They are of great import to a search for wholeness.

Plato also relates that there are "many spirits and many kinds of spirits too, and Love (Eros) is one of them." To mark a few interesting specimens that comprise a clan or family, I use the rubric of *everyday spirits*. The qualifier stresses an arena of encounter, in the midst of the daily round. Around the dwelling place, along the road, or on the job, one is met by everyday spirits in an experience of a much more powerful human nature. They are preeminently conscious forces, able to reconcile the opposing elements of ourselves. They impart an ability, enlarging and empowering us to stretch beyond a small compass. With their help, we experience ourselves at the joint of heaven and earth.

In our timebound existence, new needs emerge as old needs weary with age. The advantage of always having fresh surface exposed to influences is one that perishability holds over eternity. But time imparts a relativity that must not be overlooked. Different stages of life have different specificities and enlist different everyday spirits. Each stage has its own consciousness and voice, perception and vigor. To become whole, we must be able to listen to all. Any guidebook worth its salt must reflect this fact.

In response to demand for proper seasoning, I divide a human life in a traditional manner into four phases: the infant, the householder, the mendicant wanderer, and the sage. While other divisions are possible, the choice suits my needs. The same is true of particular everyday spirits that make their appearance. However arbitrary the selection is, our experience of them retains an inner necessity.

In addition, over each age a presiding figure reigns. I place that figure in charge of enlivening and emboldening the season of life. To meet an everyday spirit on the walk of life is no abstract event. It is an encounter with a personage, an entity, a creature, a being—a definite *something*. A figure illumines an age in the way a fragrance fills a room. The final result is a kind of calendar of everyday spirits, a month, four weeks, a lunar cycle of them. Pencil them in, but not like saints' days or days of penitence. They are days of a new order. "Be conversant with transformation," Rilke advises. Meet novelty not as a scrivener or sextant but as a devout lover. "What feeds on you/will grow strong upon this nourishment."

To say love or eros is one of the everyday spirits is to speak in love's modesty. For "the lover is an emperor; the two worlds are scattered over him and he pays no heed to the scattering" (Rumi). Other everyday spirits imitiate love in its longing for union, its caprice, its energy, and its need for disguises. As love puts on a cloak of immortality, so do they. As love overpowers the will, terrifies, startles, and deceives—and alternatively coaxes, soothes, clarifies, and foresees—so do the others. The *dynamis* that enables us to be one with our experience must bear a relation to love, or love to it, since love brings together what is separate and ends isolation of parts from the whole. Love fuels the heat of vision to incandescence and eventually leads to a kind of self-guidance. In a similar way do the many siblings of love, so that "after a long communion and common effect on behalf of the matter, a fire is suddenly kindled in the soul, as if lit by a flying spark, and henceforth can nourish itself" (Plato, *Seventh Letter*). In that magnificent moment, the clan of everyday spirits is ringed round in welcome.

PART ONE

SINDBAD

LULLABY

Is there any person who cannot be counted a seeker? Our peculiar design is like a house not yet finished, an experiment an itinerate architect tried out. What is missing—an absence—calls above the mesmerizing drone of the everyday round and at times startles us into a recognition. What we seek is very near yet very far, most great yet smallest of the small, of monumental import yet worth not a farthing, and to discover it, we require help. To whom are we to turn?

Not to the gods. They are unhelping, not just because they ceased to walk among us and grew puny. Their death was foretold by their violent birth, erupting from human consciousness full-blown, like Athena, not needing accretion, accumulation and selection, integration and denial. Of whatever name or cast, the gods give no key to the mystery of suffering. They illustrate the completed edifice, in which reflection the pain of our ignorance is magnified. Ought we to be mistrustful of perfect knowledge? A while ago, Socrates related that "none of the gods are seekers after truth. They do not long for wisdom because they are wise—and why should the wise be seeking the wisdom that is already theirs?" (*Symposium* 203e). Mistrust is the oxygen of human thought.

The all-knowing are blind and impatient when it comes to human ignorance's ignorance of itself. They may inspire or resuscitate, but the breath must be passed to us by spirits who also know the constricted chest of fear, poverty, and adversity. The gods are not exemplars of the human condition but an artist's rendering of how to elim-

3

inate its limiting strictures. The spirits who could help beings like ourselves must be both more foreign and more intimate. They must mingle with us as we mingle with our bodies, gently yet urgently. When they walk, they must walk the muck of existence with a tread as heavy as ours but uplifted. And springing up, their exuberance must not transport them to more godly realms for more than a moment. They, like we, require the ground under their heels so as to push off from earth in the direction of heaven.

Help would be easily found if the gods in this measure were helpful. They are said to be as manifold as cells in a fly's eye and to have no need of sleep. If they were substantial and obeyed the physicist's laws, great care would be needed to move about in our world, so dense would their presence be. Our desires announce a god's influence. Whenever we have wished ourselves free of limitation, a god names that condition. Which of us has the power to refrain in a stressful moment from saying, "If only I would no longer be burdened by..."? The help we need, however, comes from acceptance and embrace and not denial. Gods lend no help of their own.

Our invisible allies must share in our condition, its pain of birth, its uncertainty and peril, and its reliance on medicine, prayer, and magic. These everyday spirits are fewer than the gods, for the same reason that will is rarer than desire, hope rarer than cockiness, and remorse rarer than guilt. How everyday spirits originate does not concern me now, though unlike the gods the strength of imagination does not suffice to bring them to being. Let us say that, unlike the gods (who are creatures of time), everyday spirits have always been—or have been for as long as we have felt the need for ourselves to be. Disease brings cure; and the obstacle, its triumphal overcoming. The allies we meet in vanquishing the too-human impediments of despair, self-pity, paralysis, hatred, envy, and slough are spirits born of the twilight, the barbed wire, the no-man's-land, the desert that must be crossed.

The ancient physicians can provide a guide. They recognized that the cure, though miraculous, is never painless, and more powerful antidotes cause major upheavals in the balance of vital energies. They knew that remedies may be derived from the commonplace, substances ready-to-hand in the daily round. Such an outlook is useful. The everyday spirits whose help we seek are to be sought in the most familiar and essential of ordinary existence, the element about whom forgetfulness and memory both are miraculous—ourselves.

Is it in sleep that we come closest to ourselves? Not the sleep of
dreams, which merely subtracts the object from waking perception and
permutes the images to enact a story, but deep, dreamless sleep. We
are not the stuff dreams are made on. The dream is a bit of foreign
matter, an irritant to sleep, from which may grow a pearl or just restless discomfort. How we cling to dreams reflects our unsure grasp of
what is precious. Dreams seem to tell about ourselves the way a mirror
does when it catches us unawares. Our obscurity emerges. For dreams
tell more about the world of waking than of sleep, which lies buried,
pristine, and opaque, beneath nighttime imagery. To the great mystery, second only to (as Gilgamesh discovers, and what Sleeping
Beauty falls victim to) its cousin death, we must remember the prayer
of the lullaby, a night of undisturbed sleep:

> Lay you down now and rest
> May your slumbers be blest.

The blessing of true sleep is the infant's. To sleep like a babe is to find
sleep as it was intended to be, complete abandon. Near to the sleeping
child in a cradle hovers the first of everyday spirits. Hush, it is the lullaby. Quiet, mindful of need, we find ourselves there.

New-fallen snow barely covers frozen blades of grass. The pathway from house to woods is more recognizably itself in reshaped contours of the countryside: Roads are narrower, trees recede from
clouds, stones have new mass. First snow is the time of lullaby. Mater-
nally, it puts to rest errant urgings, itches, and tensions of desire without argument, but by a warm persuasion of total comfort. Nothing
will bother you. There is no pain, nothing to fear, no harm to come.
When you wake, everything will be as you left it. The still-life arrange-
ment of bedclothes and a few slow notes of melody are also a prayer
for the dead. Socrates proposes the pleasure of death as that of dreamless sleep everlasting. Hamlet's fear of death is the terror of recurrent
dreams. But the lullaby avows itself to side with life. The lullaby
demands one accede nightly to waters too dark for reflection. Noctural
baptism by an intelligence greater than the sum of the cogito plus our
unconscious urgings shows the true breadth of will—so rarely
glimpsed in bright daylight.

So wide and deep is will (I do not say desire) that all thought,
feeling, and sensation disappear in it as a grain of salt in the sea. Yet
when an annoying remnant of day obtrudes to leave us insomniac, a
single thought becomes insoluble. It perversely denies sleep. In sleep-

less hours of day, many unaccustomed events pass through the mind, originating like a meteor shower from a single point in the constellation of things: our refusal. Strange that lullabies are sung for the very young. The truth is that what refuses the risk of sleep appears after infancy and rises like a star with the strengthening ego. The baby needs no help to be called to sleep. Sleep overtakes the babe in the midst of a cry, a smile, a burp, and sends her sprawling, asleep, in the crib.

A snowfall works a similar wonder with leaves of the woods. If leaves refused their cover, the whole cycle—decay, reconstitution, new growth—would suffer. As attachment to schemes of the workday grows, the infant is helped by an echoic spirit, the lullaby. The word itself is a song that lulls growing preoccupation to sleep. That dying leaves sing it to themselves may be a reason for their falling. A mother who hums to knit up the raveled sleeve of care blesses her own slumber and the sleeping world's. She would, if she could, send down a blanket of snow to cover the rocky ground swiftly and deeply with its careless drifts. In the blank face is perfect repose.

In a darkened house, a single light burns. That could be a sign of industry, a task relentlessly pursued unto dawn. But no. It is a bad sign—that the sandman whose magical grains of sand close an exhausted child's eyelids has passed over without stopping. Still, to toss and turn is better with a light on than in the dark. A distance that separates desire from its object, familiar in the daily round, takes on grotesque proportions in twilight consciousness. The paralysis of being neither asleep nor awake reveals, by its negation of all possible action, how fragile our designs are. "Lord, make me to know mine end and the measure of my days, what it is; that I may know how frail I am" (Psalm 39.4). Thus sings David to the sleepless Saul. Do we hear a psalm as a lullaby for the wounded spirit? The psalm soothes. No call for quietism, it lulls a disquieted heart to the rest needed for any action. Perhaps empires have been lost for want of a lullaby. Napoleon, who could not find sleep nights before Waterloo, knew this truth. To glimpse frailty and to measure by a law of our nature the infinite expanse containing our travels: That is the hope of the psalm. To say, "I am powerless; let me sleep," frees one to be breathed in, sustained, and refreshed by the opaque power.

The lullaby is always simple. Repetition of a few notes alone suffices to repair the garment rent by open eyes. Since an infant lives but a hairbreadth from deep sleep, the smallest reminder recalls angelic existence. How angelic is the sleeping face of a baby! We must not think artists take unnecessary liberties in seeing an angel in the infant and ringing their heavenly scenes with *puti*. The undifferentiated state is as close as humankind comes to an existence beyond desire, passion, and striving.

Theologians who see birth as a fall are right only insofar as an infant, on uttering a first cry, is dropped into the sea of possibility. For angels, all is actual, every thought, every pinprick of feeling. If we may speak of it, that actuality excludes self-consciousness, because it excludes imagination. What is seen by an angel is and must be. Such seeing is not human, because it lacks the distance through which imagination moves. Spinoza calls it "seeing through the eye of eternity," *sub specie aeternitatis*. Hovering over the waters of possibility but never touching them, the angel also lacks realization. Everything being too known, nothing yields to surprise.

When intelligence returns to its organic impress during deep sleep, necessity and existence again coincide. All absence is absent, and also, as Socrates says, all love for searching things out. The fall from heaven is pregnant with birth, about which angels remain ignorant. Eyes open with sounds of suckling, the infant finds the mother's breast. She is fed. A need is nourished through satisfaction, and the babe comes in from an angelic wilderness. Hunger makes her human, just as Gilgamesh's companion Enkidu's hunger leads him to the folds of humanity. The baby is given a merest taste of possibility before returning to deep sleep, but it is enough. Permanence in the angelic void of necessaries restores energies with incomparable vitality. Who can resist abiding in the realm of deep draughts? But an infant has taken in the fleet taste of contingency and, without more, cannot endure. From now on, the way back to the angels will be blocked, imperceptibly at first, by dreams of the taste, until empyreal perception is altogether forsaken.

Fear not. The lullaby forever points to sacred emptiness, more unchanging than a Spinozistic God. Its plain melody is an invitation, intoned in semidarkness. Release, however, takes a soporific stronger than warm milk when a little pain obtrudes. Thus the drinking song, the bacchanal, comes just before the lullaby in a medley of sleep. Therein a peculiar problem arises. Wine intoxicates, besides lulling the mind to bed. Born of the grape (and hence of the earth), it may restore an inebriant to heaven, or only to heavenly imagination. A dreamer carried away by a vision of angels lies at an uncrossable distance from the source of sleep. This is the paradox of Jacob's ladder, the ladder of dreams.

Angels descend easily, but humankind ascends only through rigor of mind. To compensate, we have tried a direct assault on heaven's gates. As Babel's architects discovered, one's proximity to the upper world invokes laws of retribution to which action is not ordinarily subject. The ladder may fall to pieces, leaving disturbed dreams. The fact that drunkards babble in their cups is a clue to the real effects of drink. Only upon falling dead drunk do we indeed enjoy the sleep of a babe.

Other offspring besides the bacchanal exist as well. In Plato's garden, the story goes, Resource, "having drunk deeply of the heavenly nectar," sank into heavy sleep. There, coached at Need's hand into begetting a love of seeking truth, he awoke a father to desire. The story tells that with need's prompting our resourcefulness, all search begins. From which follows human history and the baby's. Are there, therefore, medicines too strong to soothe the pulse of imagination? Even mother's milk, no less pure than ambrosia, has its complicating side effects: the dream and its yearning for another taste. Only a simple lullaby, the unpretentiousness of its bleating sheep, directly effects entry into deep sleep without aggravation. It eschews heaven's gate and the angels' conference. It lulls us back to the source.

Under a blanket of snow, the fields sleep. "It looks as if," Frost observes, nature "had gone to sleep/Of its own stupid lack of understanding." The fields sleep because they always have. Sleep is no seasonal affair like hibernation, but a condition of organic life. And we, of that life. Angels patiently hover until dreams of life are done and they can again walk weightless over our vessel. Their constancy may never be rewarded, for humanity's yearning is real and wakeful. For them and for the meadow, snow is a great comfort.

Snow covers the country lanes one by one and puts the lights of houses out. In hamlet, village, town, and city, however, lighted windows glare at the snow with increased intensity. Cramped communal life forces men and women to defy nature and grow forgetful of the organism's needs. The city never sleeps. Its vibrancy is an ill-defined blend of dream and function, illusion and accomplishment, phantom and substance. We barely hear a lullaby for clanging pipes, screeching cars, and the staccato of telecommunications. When it snows, beauty is disregarded. The stuff is ploughed under, under city grime, and the hum (not lulling, but grating) is not softened one jot. The city is technology's refusal of comforted sleep.

Has sleep been defeated? In a country household we know, from the looks at the breakfast table, who suffered insomnia. In the city, looks are anonymous and show no intimacy except at a height of danger. No one keeps statistics on losses due to the lullaby's being throttled. The deficit is really a gain, because city philosophy stresses a missing element, and the missing element calls for a search. The country allows dreamless sleep to restore wholeness, absent in desire's daily round, and that is that. A contentment close to well-being results. In the sleepless city, things do not add up to an integer. Tastes, feels, sounds, and sights pass through a restiveness unalleviated by the night in bed. Since labor moves in unending shifts, some work in the middle of the night. *Sleeptime* is a relative term. The lullaby is another melody, quaint in spirit, of no clear purpose. Memory's image of angelic peace only increases suffering. The tense urban state has great import. Socrates avers that he cannot philosophize beyond the city walls. Only in the lullaby's absence is a question born. What is the way back?

That Socrates is right about philosophy is not a paean to urban life. Instead he embraces a spiritual discomfort necessary to a creature born to fullness and lulled back thereto at each night's parting. The lullaby sings of immortality. Is it any surprise a sleeping infant looks blissful and blissfully looks forward to sleep? Immerse her in desire, cut off the way back, and she begins to know fear. I have watched babies in their mothers' arms, words sweetly sung in their ears, fearfully refuse to close their eyes. The knowledge is beyond mere obstinacy. A germ of their diminutive willfulness lies in a fall from grace. They may be afraid of bad dreams, but the matter is more pregnant with hope.

Young children begin to obey the law of gravity. Having tasted the tree of knowledge, they turn toward their own nature. They sense the waters receding, that they may no longer find the black, nourishing body of their source. Even at this early point, an infant faces enemies that we all face—consolation and hypnosis—as well as the truth of what we want. The countryside has a clarity that the city lacks, but lacks the means to use it. The country person may dream comfortably in bed night after night, becoming victim to the condition of the earth's life. There is a contentment in watching snow cover a landscape year after year in dumb repetition, and also a capitulation. A person fed the milk of life knows a schism in his being and has grown resigned to chance happiness, a good harvest, a merry feast, or a successful marriage. Simple joys are that simple. The danger they advertise is the life of the simpleton. Earned enjoyment is otherwise. Joy is earned only when unlulled by nature's lullaby. Exeunt happy peasant, a simpleton for having fed on country fare without feeding himself. Enter urban rat whose sleeplessness has made him shrewd and resourceful and who wishes to remove its cause. Not everyone is made for happiness.

Even sleeping nature, her stones, streams, and trees that pass in and out of existence without a dream, can be incited to wakefulness. Then an immeasurable distance between basal consciousness and the daily round is eradicated. Then life can dance with death without contamination. At the call arises the Orphic song. It also belongs to sleep's medley, though it is far more dangerous than lullaby or bacchanal. The lullaby violates no prescribed limit of nature. Likewise the bacchanal, whose orgy ends in a lullaby, for nature knows and respects the violence of lust and bestiality. The opaque waters of renewal gleam sleepily below the ecstatic sexual climax.

When Orpheus's lyre moved rock and root, a balance was upset. A wall was breached. No longer of the angels' realm, earth's things became sentient beings and threatened to seek what Orpheus's contemporary, Gautama the Buddha, called "enlightenment." Gautama spoke of the humanity of nature, an idea that we find self-contradictory. The great workman, the boddhisatva, was he who postponed his own attainments until "every blade of grass" found its buddha-mind. When Orpheus conferred locomotion on stones, the effect was to advance the cosmic clock a few hours. An accelerated rate would have ended history and our local epoch before the next sunrise. Such foreshortening of an individual's quest is unnatural.

Put another way, Orpheus discovered a way to heaven that did not pass through deep sleep. A wayfarer could wakefully ply the seas back to the source and wakefully contact the great whole. The prescription is entirely new. Like a mother her swaddling babe, we must encircle the fullness of our being, from an inchoate, formless state to a most elevated clarity. Dream, dreamlessness, and waking perception each in turn must yield to the cock's crow. Shortcuts are forbidden. Finding this out, Orpheus sang, and nature came alive to his music. His waking cry penetrated even to the upper world, and nature rebelled. Hence the violent and unequivocal manner of Orpheus's death.

"We ought to offer a cock to Asclepius." Socrates' last words on passing from life to death are a reminder of the need for health care. Perfection of an infant's health permits the lullaby to work. An imperfection of ours eventually calls for the dirge, a lullaby in a minor key. Deep dreamless sleep is a draught designed to restore care. Dawn refreshes the eyes washed by sleep's waveless intensity.

Yet a day may fall quickly into dis-ease. A wrinkle so slight we feel it predestined may upset the peaceful morning light. A dirgeful anxiety attending the less than perfectly healthy awakens. With its drone, we stand in the muck of possibility, trying to allow a cross-fertilization to take place. As I understand it, we must cast a little light upon the sea of blackness and behold a lotus rise to the surface. The cogito must be extinguished, and its shards scattered over the waters from which dreams are born. The very act of impregnation transforms our being utterly and takes us far from our first subject, the lullaby. Suffice it to say now that Orpheus's crime, awakening nature, made it seem as though one was able to love at will. If a sleeping world obeys me, then surely my heart must. But the truth, when painfully sought, shows the opposite. The will to love involves a surrender of lover to beloved. That is the way the world works, and that is why one cannot assault heaven's gates. And surrender is precisely a mother's lullaby as she sings it softly near her infant's sleeping face.

2

THE BLINK

Follow an infant's gaze backward. Open eyes take everything *in* yet see no thing. Vision still belongs to the angels, a fact forgotten when the miracle of sight is forgotten. It leaps over time and space to the other side of a valley where evening mist rises over a lake. What an infant sees bathes in the waters of life that cling without radiance. In proportion and shape her eyes are like ours—yet they are not. They are enclosed by an aura of the suprahuman, since they differ from our eyes in one critical respect. A baby's eyes do not blink.

Rarely are we aware of ourselves blinking. Yet several times a minute the lid closes over the seeing organ, leaving us alone in sightless, opaque existence. We make special note in others of an unblinking gaze. It is mark of truthfulness, and the one in truth remembers days of child's play, back to a time of infancy. Truth itself does not waver, because it is perfectly mutable. It is master of both naiveté and artifice and always bold when it comes to lies. A con artist, if truly an artist, possesses a direct gaze for the same reason. He does not depart from truth telling, since truth, as we know, steals secrets from the heart and is indiscreet about hidden treasure. That an inebriant may also look with a steady stare demonstrates the truth-seeking power of the grape. His gaze becomes unsteady when the other, deeper soporific power calls. Then his eyes close to truth.

All three—truth teller, confidence man, and drunkard—express without distance their moving desire. They imitate an infant who has not learned delay, deferment, and difference. Men and women who

blink perceptibly, by contrast, do so because of manners, self-con-
sciously or unconsciously adopted. Reticence, I would say, exemplifies
a mannered behavior that affects a blinking gaze. A reticent person's
reserve is reflection, unduly stressed. One turn toward a darkened, disquieted interior, and the object of pursuit is lost. In all events, the cardinal rule of agency is discarded—deliberately to locate oneself in a
field of action. The corollary never quite trusts that willy-nilly one is
there. Thus, the blink is precisely the shadow that falls between
thought and act. Aristotle placed choice by means of reason at the center of the human stage. He thereby installed the blink unwittingly as a
symbol of humanity, since to choose is first to turn toward the interior.
A reticent one—Hamlet, for instance—blinks before speaking, in
order to cause logic to predetermine his words.

Truth can seem inhuman and inhumane. Truths like a beloved's
sudden death, or that of a heroic project, we greet with unblinking
eyes. Truths of grotesque proportion, massacres, genocides, tortures,
treacheries, and colossal ingratitudes produce similar responses—for
different reasons. We are then numbed to truth. As Sindbad, hero of
infancy, recalls, the embrace of one's truth is never the same, because
truth is always bent.

A contrary argument regarding the blink also exists. Some say a
blinkless stare derives from the natural, not the human, world. A babe
inherits the philogenetic relic and discards it when she grows ontolog-
ical. A snake's stare is nonhuman and unblinking. It is wily, fierce, and
treasonous, beguiling our submissive side to taste the fruit and know
the distance of desire. A crow has a cagey, though not hypnotic, stare.
Anxiety in a cat's eye and blankness in a cow's are also documented.
Each animal totem, the argument goes, is to be lived through and
dropped as a blinking truth emerges of ourselves.

Animals and humanity coalesce in a single drop in the undifferentiated state. The proof is that a well-sung lullaby puts a serpent to
sleep. After that, nature mimics humankind, as Aesop teaches. A toad
puffs up with pride, a wolf puts on disguises to infiltrate its prey, and a
dog loses its bone to greed. A mirror is held up, and we see ourselves.
But on occasion we see the mirror itself—what lies behind the brute-
ness with which perception is framed or the savagery of our eyes. That
allows us to feel how we claw at the world, tear it to shreds, and glut-
tonize ourselves on its pieces—unlike the unblinking infant who lets
things in without feeding on them.

But this is rare, and more often the matter is simply reticence and reflection. In a blink, we both belong and do not belong to the animal world. Beasts' unblinking eyes testify to their knowledge that, upon sleep, they will find their way back to the life within life. Our blink hides that truth.

In the blink of an eye, we encounter the problem of trust. The problem, as Descartes saw, is of the cogito—the thought-logged ego. Cogito and problem are one, since ego is both maker and resolver of problems. The fact raises unsettling anxiety, idealism, or madness. Once authority lies in reason and the reasoning will, can we trust the world to agree with our deductions? As a prime instance, an inference from thought-play to the fact that I exist. Descartes's solution is a solemn joke, as rich as Plato's exclusion of the tragedians from the republic. He tells that reticence itself, the ego's delay of self-expression, is the guarantor of being. The ego is driven to thinking about things. Proof of existence lies in thinking about desire, passion, fear, and even thought, wherein I reflect on its factuality and being. Not proven is how I exist beyond the momentary distance—which lends my life the property of blinking off and on like a firefly on a July night. Only God (whose existence suffers similar proofs) can stop the eye from blinking.

Berkeley, also interested in the eyeblink, worried about the world's interruptedness. Did it disappear altogether from truth and existence whenever eyelids involuntarily drooped over eyeballs? The query is of a despair of trust. Who believes everything is whisked away, other than one overcharged with thought? He or she who deliberates over what morsel to choose and finds the platter withdrawn. The blink interrupts fixity yet is part of the mortal frame. Only God and his immortal angels do not blink: The world's continuance rests on matchless vision. Thus Berkeley refutes Descartes.

Blink after blink, our eyes open to a field different only by a shade—a bit more green, less fogbound, grass bent over, a deer now at the tree line. An angel sees only what is preserved and worthy: the field as eternal canvas. An infant sees a permanence of change: Addition or subtraction yields no difference. An animal record of brute differences has a beauty of its own. A person given to dreams and dreamlike perceptions wonders what occurs during sight's occlusion. He or she peers into the shadows. Reticence makes her its victim. He retains an image, but is memory to be trusted? Who has played the parlor game of remembering an object on the tray, only to be deceived? The ancients' *ars memoralis* is a defense against this weakness but does not annul the fear. The ancients did not question memory even after executing the bard whose memory had grown fallible.

For us, memory holds the scales of justice by which to tare the metaphysical weight of a blink. Is memory trustworthy? A gazing infant at the breast closes her eyes. When done, she looks across the room and blinks. She is moved, her clothes are changed, she is carried to the next room. One thing interrupts another. Relocation and rearrangement occur. Locomotion to and from a desired object is the first teacher. No wonder Hobbes identifies freedom with the body's free movement. An infant quickly learns she is subject to the logic of desire even before knowing desire itself. The strange, unforgettable lesson takes hold in the organism's behavior. It goes a long way toward explaining the modern fascination with schemata and programs rather than with actual doings. Memory is a table or tablet. A table itself is immune to blinking (the form of interruption), however many real elements change, since it is the form of forms. The drift away from contingency—or attraction to the immutable—is none other than the displaced call of dreamless sleep. The everyday world puts on a cloak of immortality. The cogito devises its version of forbidden knowledge of the other, the mindless one. Mind-invented necessity is changeless, flat, and stale in relation to ever-changing necessity heralded by the lullaby.

I digress, which is relevant. To digress is to follow a thought that interrupts another like snow flurries heading toward the same field. I repeat the lateral motion that infant experiences while transported through, and rearranged in, space. *That* indirection is delay. Through constantly repeated interruption—necessary to its hygiene and well-being—a baby learns that no desire is satisfied to the utmost and that satiety and want are both undesirable extremes. Through these Aristotelian means, she is introduced to the mathematics of hope.

Let me backtrack. Another clue to the problem of trust is given by Mesmer. The wide-eyed, unblinking stare of a hypnotic is easily caricatured. A person under the influence of a blinkless trance may perform outlandish acts, walking on fire without fear in the post-hypnotic state. In the eclipse of self-will (by the hypnotist's brilliant skill), one's ocular habits revert to infancy. Infancy of consciousness must lie right under the skin, since we may be suddenly mesmerized by strident lights, soft colors, intense smells, sharp sounds—elements of the daily round. The technique mimics a lullaby with the aid of mirrors. A connection between self-will and interrupted sight discloses a hidden aspect of our being. Fear lurks in the blink's momentary blindness. It is no obvious fear, attributed to the primitive mind, of darkness per se. A dark night hides the object of fear. It then is uncovered by pratfall or accident, the way that we come across a ditch, a marauder, or our insecurity. If we flinch, we blink—adding darkness to darkness but activating the reflex for counterattack. For her own protection, the infant blinks when startled without once learning how. The capability is not yet fear, but a mold into which it can be poured; of this I speak later.

Darkness does not bring comfort, but neither does it leave us unprepared. A hero takes flight under cover of darkness or works his heroic rescue. The ego is valiantly defended. No, fear beneath the blink is of interruptedness itself. Dreamless sleep, the ultimate repose toward which all paths of conquest lead, is repeatedly broken by dreams. So too the small glass of concentrated power focused on the world, the lens through which we attenuate a will greater than ours. Break after break rouses fear that the dream begins anew. The vacuous self-will that Mesmer unveils shows us to be afraid of losing what is deemed untrustworthy, ourselves.

Sometimes a lethargy overtakes us in the midst of a stride. Call it "autohypnosis" if you want. Desire is emptied, a hold on the reins of action is let loose. We become as a child, unblinking. Fearing expectations thwarted, we greet the state with *ennui*—"the unpurged images of day recede" (Yeats). In *tedium du monde*, dreams have license to drift like floaters over a retina or snow past a kitchen window. The formless state, free from motive, without rhyme or reason, moves nearer. Passion, fear, and mistrust are rendered innocuous. "I am too bored to blink," goes the saw that places boredom beside truth. What can interrupt boredom? A new song, a new suit of clothes, new wine, a new love. In the blink of an eye, the new year appears in castanets and thrown rice. One who broods misses the celebration. A fall into possibility is apt to be missed due to blinking, brooding ways. Reticence's niggardly trust mistrusts even its own desires, which accounts for why the object fails to satisfy. But at year's cold dark midnight, the spheres turn, dreams dissolve, and a transluminous body of water disappears. Once again, we rely on forgetfulness, trying like the poor farmer of the fairy tale to recall the map to the treasure garden.

A stale copper taste of despair rises when interruption ceases to interrupt. What really is known of the rupture in the established order that the blink heralds? The child is familiar with creatures of the *Augenblinkt*. They are creatures of trust—for that is how this everyday

spirit dresses—who make their appearance in the space of a blink.
Faeries, elves, leprechauns, dwarfs, and some wizards exist in the spacious realm. A child's knowledge is a simple thing. She knows the world will
not be swallowed by interruption. We do not call the creatures "magical." Turn a leaf up, and a sylph is there; feel under the pillow, and find
the tooth fairy's home: Their kind lives in the undoubting look and
dies in the doubt of a second look. Life for us consists of a glance
repeated. What does that leave? The staid testimony of mnemonic disclosure antidotes despair. Belief is forged only by holding on to much
evidence. *Augenblinkt* beings are magical because their advent lies
outside of reticence and logic. The account books that have built cities
are of no use. Let fear go, and kick that stone over without flinching.
Any child knows elven wishes get real results.

Life goes by in the blink of an eye. A pessimist pictures the babe
already in grim combat with death. Each drooping eyelid presages the
final closure when coins for Charon are set in place. A philosopher's
temptation is to misread final causes for efficient ones, as the logicians
say, *post hoc ergo propter hoc.* It blinds observation, since death is when
we run out of blinks. The fundamental truth of mortality is not to be
blinked. Recall the unblinking eyes of a dying soldier who gives for-
giveness to friend and enemy alike. He is released from interruption
and turns back to what suffers no interruption, dreamless sleep. No
more does the bright sun make him blink. Nor does he blink tears of
joy or sorrow from his eyes. A dust mote, a speck of sand, a sneeze,
heat from a fire, the aroma of camphor: None affects him any longer.
The blink is the first stop in earthly metaphysics. Each subsequent
blink marks another station, of fear, embarrassment, infatuation, pain,
pretension, or plain fatigue. The magical invention of memory is a map
of discovery. From the voyager's viewpoint, death redoes boundaries,
necessitating a new survey. Memory subsides to its organic substra-
tum, then to a single cosmic point. Death is no first principle of a
blinking baby, but a reversion to nonbeing.

An infant's open gaze. How silent we are before it. Thought
comes to a stop until preoccupation begins anew. Could it be that the
blink foreshadows reason, cast backward in dawn light? In anticipa-
tion, an infant blinks. The swirl of thought to which she will be subject
moves nearer. Soon other gifts will be needed.

3

THE GIFT

The beggar is poor and in need. Every night, at the conclusion of a new tale of tribulation, he is given a hundred sequins by Sindbad the Sailor. Sindbad's riches are well earned. But he would grow mean and miserly with them kept to himself. Therefore, to recount their discovery is a gift demanding a second giving.

At a birthday party the storyteller sometimes arrives with trinkets to pass around. The same spirit prompts guests to cry, while presents are unwrapped, "Speech, speech!" to the celebrant. Opening an abundant larder, a fabulist makes an additional payment. Momentum of habit is forgetful that speeches must be paid for. To fill others' ears, we must provide a token of gratitude. To pay thus is to pray, to remember a prayer of speaking. The silent count of coins foreshadows a count of vesper bells when thought takes flight.

A young child never lives far from double exchange. Speaking is born of a terrifying necessity of desire. Vico, Condillac, and Rousseau were obsessed with the origin of language. They meant speech in its infancy, implying that language is the work of spirits, not the gods who have no childhoood. First words are commands and imperatives. Before they come, cries, growls, cooings, squeals, and shrieks vocalize body pantomime. Flailing limbs, grasping fingers, puckered lips, and contorted faces are expressive, but not as speech. They do not require the odd doubled payment, since they involve no indirection. We tip a messenger boy who rings the bell, but not a guest who is let in. Thus "Mama" and "Dada" come with the gift, a smile, an effusion of a grace,

19

a secret breath that lightens the atmosphere. Those in proximity breathe
in the word. Infant speech exhales a presence that nourishes inner life.
Breath itself, of child or crone, partakes of the same gift on top of gifts
Sindbad bestows on paupery.

Each child is monarch with rights and privileges of command.
Royalty is childlike in decree, without reticence, and certain. A child's
is a true inheritance (and not usurped or gained by conquest), and, like
the sovereign, a child is cognizant of the law of command—particularly, command of audience. Attention immediately is attracted to her
in any gathering. A child is privy to the power by which she is granted
her fiefdom. In accord with the will of the world, her might cannot be
measured by adult standards. Apparent deficiencies (in language and
locomotion) are disguises of her play in court. Hers is a high station,
though the gift of lots, given not by gods but by angels, is undoubled,
singular, and unique—and beyond present interest. Suffice it that
Sindbad is like a child in that he honors his divvy without a grudge.

A clear conscience is needed for double gift giving. If the ground
is overgrown, a pruning knife may open one to the spirit. The edge
must be adequate to the end. Hamlet knew that a play's the thing to
catch the conscience of the king. In that day, players customarily dis-
tributed prizes to an audience before performance. Artists' sensibilities
were then mindful of Sindbad's practice. The playbill survives as a sole
relic of this thoughtful practice. Playacting itself may be a fossil of
childhood games of pirate, explorer, householder, doctor,...or king.
We reinvent knowledge of innocence to remind us of amnesia. An
infancy of conscience keeps a simple account sheet for gifts, given and
received.

Playacting invests an idea of the world with indubitable reality.
Here is a tunnel to the center of the earth, where a ferocious troll lives.
You must throw him a sop if you wish to pass. A child succeeds at what
Descartes schooled himself to do, willing suspension of belief. Play and
dream resist a self-willed discipline, for Descartes was stymied by
dream elements that haunted his method of doubt. Put another way,
he resisted telling himself a story about his existence. Child's play does
not distinguish real from make-believe (though a child can, by stopping the game), whereas we, who get no repose from dreams, do.
Dreams preoccupy thought as vague associations, and disbelief blocks
the miracle of letting them go their own way. Interpreters dress
dreams in adult suits to give dreams a civility that dreams lack. Dreams
are child desires uninformed as to rules of reticence. They strive for an

object, wander around it, whimsically give it out, get sidetracked, replaced, or revalued, in the blink of an eye. A dream itself is a form of payment. It belongs to a system of exchange, the same system as does the story. The ritual bedtime story is not merely a convenient way to quell a child's frenzy. The lord of the day bears gifts for the lord of the night. He repeats the story to himself as his head meets the pillow. Now the gift of dreaming is made possible.

Double exchange—a gift bestowed in payment for telling a story—belongs to a forgotten ethic. It is not appeasement for jealous and angry gods whose inventions (language included) Prometheus stole. Sindbad demonstrates how to give willingly and in gratitude, not out of fear of retribution. In play, abundance, not scarcity, prevails. Child and storyteller refer to no calculus of consequences. "Will I run out of yarn to spin?" is never a serious consideration. Yet player remains pragmatist. One pays in coin for a mate or an audience for the simple reason that one's desire, and not the other's, is being pursued. Double exchange is an honest confession of who stands to profit.

Nowadays Sindbad scarcely enters into our lullabies. Labor has displaced play and the niggardly single exchange of work, the double exchange. The cost of labor is measured in work hours. It takes that much time to wrench the commodity, a chair, a bowl, or a dressing gown, from nature's raw bounty. Valuation is based, according to Locke, on compensation. (Psychologists redeploy the notion in describing dreams as thwarted desires.) To make up for hardship of manufacture, we exact gold from a purchaser. This is only justice. A child plays with the idea, using buttons or pebbles, keeping track by an obscure, unaccountable reckoning—but then paying a customer to take the merchandise away! Infant justice applies to all toys. Toys are never bought, since they have no use value. They are gifts or are just there, which is the same thing. Admission to theatrical performances is a way station along the way from double to single exchange. Lear's fool forever gives away baubles with the scenes that he stages. In his generosity lives a more primordial economy that governs speech. When we harken to its spirit, our step is buoyed up.

I am struck by a child's outstretched hand, holding a toy for a companion. She tells the story of how her favorite teddy bear was born. The account places sympathy dead center in a moral order, as Hume does. His is an ethic of childhood. The reach for power—the adult ethic—is concealed because power is possessed. A child dispenses things in accordance with the same laws Sindbad obeys. Each occasion of speech, each utterance, tells a story in the same way an open door tells of a welcome hearth. Spirit is revealed in its humble work, sweeping, stirring, feeding, tidying. The peculiar local vibration of one's sound discloses willy-nilly the hidden reality—should ears be able to hear. How prudent the ethic is. For a speaker who recognizes this manifest everyday spirit, gold is the guarantee and a cheap one at that.

A fee for self-revelation must be tendered freely. Otherwise words become strident objects, signs pointing only to each other in competition for attention. They lack real command and order us about like supervisors. They—and we—join the workplace. In the shop, necessity replaces need, and desire is ingraciously pursued, since its end cannot be had the child's way. It is fast food wolfed down at lunch break.

The tablecloth is as white as snow. Party favors are set, candles burn. Snow outside covers the boots, and stars, if visible, would show constellations of the child's nativity. A storyteller is seated in the circle. She has passed around her gifts—shells, dried bones, birds' feathers—and is about to begin. "What story would you like to hear?" "Tell me about me," the child says. "Tell me about things I once did."

The question of initiation is an early favorite. A child takes the storyteller's offering, opens the door to her playhouse, and finds somebody there. Who? Asking brings a recollection. The first initiation is into history.

Properly speaking, history is initiator of the individual. Force of tradition is the hand that molds clay into a useful vessel. A life within takes the shape and holds it. Most often, the first is the final act. Sometimes, years after games have ceased, an adult will seek initiation into eternity. To an unforeseen call comes an unknown response. Neither is greater than the other, for *I* fits the void as eyeball the empty socket. A child senses throughout shifting panoramas what Hume was unable to find by reason: a something that, though it may not endure temporal pageantry, is worthy of an enduring story. "But play, you must, a tune beyond us, yet ourselves" (Wallace Stevens). The self—the one subject of the *his-storia*—is no treatise on human nature, as the reticent Hume supposed. "Tell me what I did" demands a catalogue of the world's things (as Homer supplied an inventory of ships) as well as of deeds of humankind that involve those things. To retell the story of liberation is a storyteller's ongoing work.

"Tell me about me" recites an alphabet of the psyche. First initiation, into passion, desire, fear, and the accumulated anecdotes of climate, craft, and geography, entertains in a specific way. It rouses imagination from dreamy slumber, calling it forth through device (as Aladdin his lamp) to illuminate a cave. It transforms an infant's relation to the angelic plenum, dreamless sleep, much more than all gustatory delights. It substantiates a belonging and a longing to belong to herself alone, separate from nurturing maternal nature in whose bosom she sleeps. She has become the once and future monarch. Through a story is she born.

It works the other way too. A sovereign undergoing initiation rediscovers the mystery of childhood and is transformed. An unknown mendicant or dervish who has the ruler's ear leaves her a demigod, demagogue, or all agog. We have grown distrustful of such guidance as a Rasputin gives. But Scheherazade? Through her skill, she creates a beguiling tale of intricate beauty that shows the sultan his barbarous practice, restores his latent humanity, and thereby saves the kingdom. The story is a maze, one yarn nesting inside another, and Scheherazade is the one who opens a brute heart with the keen edge of the sultan's honor. Recall Scheherazade's daring gamble. She must be beheaded if the sultan commands, and will live only as long as her story does. Her telling is a matter of life or death. The story nevertheless remains a child's play. Only now, the tyrant must be killed if the tale is to go on. How to kill him without killing the sultan? Her choice reveals love's flaw (for the sultan was a known lover), which is needing to know the ending. Her life—the storyteller's risk—depends on spinning an endless yarn endlessly. If she is true, the tyrant will die before the story is over.

Love whose strength is boundless is obscured by lower natures. Accordingly, a teller's work of truth and promise is infected with deep superstition. An exact form must be followed, with beginning, middle, and end in right order. If not, death comes at dawn. We must not be surprised at the storyteller's prayer: "Thou wilt prolong the king's life, and his years as many generations" (Psalm 61.6). To pray for a good hearing is a child's subtle suffusion of joy, transmuted and directed heavenward. A king's enjoyment is life itself, and death of his beloved is no different from an execution at the hands of the lord high executioner. Thus the sultan remembers.

The story is about to begin. Once upon a time, there was an unjust king....We are gathered unto a history before recollection and initiated into ways immemorial of humankind. From loving waters the lotus rises. That the story is of love makes one further point clear. Its double gift is an action, not a memory. At dusk we may come together in honor of some great personage, to toast him and to reminisce about his accomplishments. Anecdotes partake of the story but idolatrize sentiments. A toast, however, belongs to the ethic of double exchange. After dinner conversation with the family, some forebear is changed through reminiscence through a newly invented role in the drama of lineage. The family album under lamplight becomes the tree of humanity. We are edified on hearing how an angry man struggles justly or a victim falls to self-pity and succumbs. How love imparts a knowledge, sometimes cruel, then reveals an unknown energy within that frees us to obey it. Listening, obedience itself, sensitizes conscience. A story's ultimatum is no less ultimate than a monarch's. Speak and be heard, or suffer to die. Threat of choice gives particular desires, passions, ideas, and ideologies their human meaning, their sole meaning, through the act of double exchange. That a child intuits Rumpelstiltskin's motive or Cinderella's valor—and accepts the storyteller's gift—shows how meaningless patterns of the daily round efface the etchings within the heart.

4

GRIP

Being's immense power does not loosen an infant's grip. Watch as miniature hand is prodded by maternal finger. Muscles flex with knowledge. The fist closes over an object, holding it from release into the ambient world. When gently shaken, the finger gains no freedom. What meaning belongs to the phenomenon? Angels do not know it. Their insubstantial bodies are able to keep, without gripping, the deep preserve of things. Is curiosity roused when a sleeping infant visits their region?

Unbroken slumber, when the farthest outposts of the ego have forsaken their watch, leaves a body willful and animate. Even near by death's near province, it rebels against uniformity, changeless peace, and perpetual tranquility. No wonder an inner daimon is attracted to pure physical vitality. To the call of earthbound life comes the mystery of response. In deep coma, lives do an impossible feat of moving limbs and lips and even speaking. The everyday spirit of the grip does not move aside even for nonbeing. Such is the enormous power of this guide. A spirited grasp is the very metaphor for will itself. The beauty of facelessly white snow is rivaled by a single trace of footprints doggedly climbing a hillside. Some person walks into night. Let us follow.

To speak literally of our "grip" on things is to let assumption go. Grip precedes an urge to make, concoct, or create: *Homo faber* is a child of *Homo hendens*. An infant's initiatory exercise in the prehensile hand follows after lips seize on to nipple. Attachment to objects derives

25

from the nutritive function. To take food in first means to take hold of it by lip or grip. Otherwise nearness is of angels, a ghostly, idealist affair that does not sustain life any more than does a picture of a loaf of bread.

The grasping gesture is writ deep in the nature of things. Aristotle read it and presumed that it illustrated the way properties adhere to being. His logic can be extended. A similar action is required with respect to other kinds of nourishment, air and impressions. The flex of the diaphragm is a way of gripping the wind, and more active than sail and propeller, which merely stand in a force's way. Similarly, Descartes saw the brain as a subtle muscular valve that lays hold of lively perceptions. The rest passes as in a dream. Others portray a literal gripping of hands taking place in the intelligible realm. Old drawings of an homunculus that manually sorts mental images dealt with the same subject. Such artists know the hand is quicker than the mind.

Will must have its place. What sticks by itself is dust, lint, and grime. The issue has an obverse. Payment must be made, effort exacted, before the mind's vision becomes ours. Not to grasp experience is to suffer a malnutrition whose cure is prayer and whose continuance is the sickness unto death.

An infant's grip keeps a gentle vigilance that prevents things from slipping away. The breast and the mother's finger stay close enough to work their miracle of nourishment. Force of separation otherwise presides, as it does on a grand scale in the flight of stars one from the other. An infant shows that in human terms the sole unifying power is the body. To become one means to become one body, prolonged and radiant. A house exemplifies a unity of beings under one roof, just as the city unites many homes under provision of necessities and communication. The idea of action at a distance, when it means anything, means two distant bodies are cells of a larger one and so affect each other like a tear affects a heart. Spinoza concluded that all beings are cells in God's body or (the same thing) nature's. Apart from grip, natural phenomena have the fleetingness of dreams, with the same effect one dream object has on another. The thought may disturb sleep not merely because a universal sea change excludes us. People find the grip of a higher power uncomfortable because it evokes fear, resignation, or surrender. On a whim, the gods transformed Daphne into an oak tree. She, like Job, had done nothing of offense. Such a divine vigil has a grip on even invisible, incorruptible motives and leaves no one safe.

In human terms, love holds an infant's lips to the breast. Love is the first and universal term in an evolving consciousness. The object of desire is thereby awakened and gains autonomy. It stimulates other attributes, of love, artifice, enchantment, and seduction. Calculation is supposed by each new power. An infant, wanting more, grows playful and devious. Hansel and Gretel grasp in their hands a cunning greater than a witch's. Measurement enters the transaction since the desired cup may outrun its natural measure. Resourcefulness fills the excess and knows exactly how much is got. *More*, meaning more than needed, is a germ of greatness.

Overstepping, outdoing, or transcending announces itself as a possibility in action and later in word, *mine*. Self-importance—coloration of the cogito—derives from limit. What satisfies the limit, quantity and recurrence, and what does not, excess or deficit, become known. Measure is a giant step in unraveling infant consciousness from her matrix. Maternal milk no longer exists solely as a taste or gustatory sensation, but now exists as a thing in its own right. What is able to stop the force of deduction? Limit defines an object and presents itself as an independent source of existence, equal to the limitless. Henceforth, belief sets humanity as the measure of all things and the divine as secondary in stature. By our grip shall our humanity be known.

I jump too quickly ahead, being in the grip of thought. Let us first examine grip per se. A child's mixes deftness with urgency. This is a clue. She has yet to learn that gripping the implement or assailant too long or too fiercely leads to overthrow. We are shackled by our own grip. The surfeit the infant seeks is not from greed but from attachment to a pleasant sensation. A mountain lake is not greedy when spring thaw remakes its shores. Deprivation subverts nature and brings cunning. Grip is changed into a wily possession of things due as a matter of course. Need is ancillary to the rule, the Me, that embodies a principle of ownership. Is any sign of the proprietor more potent than grasping fingers? Recall the persistence of the grip in an infant—long after the mother slipped away—to see that an object's insubstantiality, unbelievability, or perverseness has no purchase. A hand closes on itself. Aspirations are of nightmarish proportion, megalomaniacal and fascistic. A hand also defines the role of a householder on the daily round of work and leisure, silence and conversation, burial and discovery. Grip is an answer to poverty, resourcefulness itself.

In the play of tempos, a mind moves more slowly than a hand. The differential explains much of what passes as magic, including how the little tailor squeezed blood from a stone while the giant could not. (The Magi, too, carried gifts whose object the mind has since vainly sought.) How much more quickly does a grip learn cunning than its most able pupil, a mind. That the ego is concentrated in flexed fingers is, however, an idea deemed absurd by an intellect. Mind's image of birth is more godly—Athena explodes in full majesty from the split skull of Zeus. Absurdity is what thought cannot get a grip on. By analogy, a flexed hand is high above the thinking organ in regard to certainty. Indubitability is what mind seeks. Yet a most potent sign of certitude is a clenched fist raised for all to contemplate. There is certainty in the purest and surest of passions, anger.

Recall how an infant grips angrily at the inevitable delay of desire. I have seen the most placid of babies clench fists in wrath at a slight maternal inadvertence. Her color is livid, her cry furious, her grip taut with righteousness. Soothing brings no relief. Her anger is objectless. A tantrum is excusable by virtue of the infant's obliviousness. We thereby disregard the fact that anger, first of all emotions, appears without object, hence without solace. In anger's grip, the child is not guided by her own in the face of life's interruptedness, but succumbs to its fits. Seeds of hysteria as well as rapture lie in such surrender.

A difficult point emerges. That mentality (together with the ego and its gravitational pull) is an offspring of ire is an unthought thought. Ancient tongues placed the roots nearer one another: *menis*, Greek for "anger," and *mens*, Latin for "mind" or "intent." In Sanskrit, *manas*—from which *human* is derived—means both "spirit" and "anger." *Menis* is the first word of the first chapter in the sublime *Iliad*. Pride, Aristotle's tragic flaw, is only an aftereffect of anger, a cooled crust of personality, much as a volcano's cone is a relic of an eruption. A hero raises a clenched fist to signify a victorious intent. Even as cunning a device as the sail needs wind to drive it. Anger, be it scathing, seething, or cold as ice, *directs* thought. In anger we leave home. Anger undoes mind's love of images, its desire to merge as one with them (in the dream), and thrusts thought out willy-nilly at an object. "Here we must make separation/And go out through a thousand miles of dead grass" (Pound). The result is a new orientation toward earth.

A child's first firm intention, its willfulness, derives from "angry thoughts." Rage is father of wrathful design or aggression, which predominates whenever man meets man in trade, culture, or war. Mind's pedigree does not therein spring from a low place. To irritate nature is to cause the pearl of technology to be created. Anger irks. Since a natural repose of mind is in an undifferentiated state, anger transmutes fullness of being into practical skills. Silence is given the word; an eye, its distance; and grip, its tools. Hunting, building, the crafts, the trades, combat, art, and language are progeny. Without anger and a mind galvanized to action, desire would be a phantom brush of an angel's wing. Our fiery dispositions would be placid and negligible, dark brow of a hillside under which we dream. Perhaps this fire was Prometheus's, who stole from the jealous gods to order to give to humans.

What is able to placate? A mood of aggression, born of grip, must be returned from its cerebral throne to the fleshy fold. Otherwise, one relies on an older physiognomy—redheaded is impetuous, fair-haired slow to ire, a dark one opaque in purpose—and thinks the worst. With a handshake, grip extended to the other, one exposes what lies hidden within a hand—nothing. I come unarmed; set your guard at ease. An empty, decontracted grip welcomes the other as no other means can. Suspicion is quieted, and a basis for reciprocal relations established. From the primal act follows all communal life: the hunt, the field, and the city. Should treachery ensue, double vindication is warranted, one for violence and one for a deceptive greeting.

Caveat salvator. For a handshake exposes more than a concealed weapon. It disarms anger by revealing deep springs of dispositions. No one stays hidden behind a handshake. We meet the grip of courage, resoluteness, cowardice, greed, fear, and insecurity. Liar, fop, and spy are exposed no less than the knight steadfast and pure. As one's grip is one's hold on the world, so each grip holds a world entire and complete. Compare the handshake of a blacksmith or carpenter to that of a surgeon or painter. Since a handshake is sudden intimacy, an encounter within one's body, temptation may occasion a secret sign. A slight manipulation of the grip counts as a password, acknowledgment of shared knowledge, admission into an esoteric school. Fleshy palm holds in its breadth no less than a mind does—and more, since it is able to surrender its grasp to another's with a humble heart.

Is it greed that freezes a will when we cannot open the grip? A phantom fear that Aesop's dog knew affects us all. The animal carried a bone in its mouth. Seeing another reflected in the brook it crossed, it feared its possession was only second best. The apprehension is that our grip does not suffice. Actuality remains a confused state as long as we mistake image for our reality. Idealism grips us when our possessions seem wrought in heaven. Reticence is reborn when we do not share goods with others who share our need. Who is guilty of this sin? An infant who holds nourishment in her hands knows sufficiency as well as exchange.

When belief grows fixed, grip is projected onto the world and thereby compromised. Its usefulness—once to express vital determination—now holds a hammer, picks up a pen, lifts a child to her bed. The ego cannot help but inflate or deflate itself, given an immensity that lies beyond it. Aesop, cast into a slave's lot, knows reticence. The story of the frog and the ox recollects an inherent reaction to largeness. Swelling to infinity, we rupture a hold on our special finitude. A study of medicine thus begins with grip and its weaknesses. Human illness follows when craving demands protection against the unknown. Addiction is Shiva's, god of destruction's, wrathful face. It walks the land, countryside and city alike. Idealism is the grip of anger striving to undo itself. Is there an amulet against the hegemony of attachments? Can we pick up a stick without being used by our intention? Will ego take its proper place once our purpose is revealed? The forms of prayer are countless and of many faces. None is more efficacious than a grip's simple, uncomplicating willfulness to grasp and be grasped by the willing world.

5

VOWS

A muddy brook appears as a stain just beneath snow's white surface. A new season has been promised and must come. In the older image of the gods, time devours his children for fear they will destroy him as he did his father before him, heaven. Wrathful thought lives to do unto a future what we were done unto by a past. Yet the rivulet gains body and begins to flow on its own accord. Snow melts and adds its substance to the unending accumulation of the sea. Eros again triumphs over an urge to eternalize an object, or to trivialize it.

Love shows our lack of beauty and compassion, itself being as Plato says, "harsh and arid, barefoot and homeless, sleeping on the naked earth, in doorways, or in the very streets beneath the stars of heaven" (*Symposium* 203c). Though time fixes and makes rigid a rush of life, what animates its vengeful spirit is our own vengefulness. Nietzsche saw this clearly. Thought may gain its direction from the passion of anger. Two things follow. A negative value is not necessary. And the fruit is still in question. Surely, a new, freer attitude is possible. No longer to rectify our grip, we move forward with a presence and a wish to embody a human destiny. Ice unfreezes, and water does not stagnate for long. A future lies in this direction.

In actual practice, uncountable difficulties call forth a great ingenuity. In my neighborhood is a cavern in which sheets of glacial ice pass summer without melting. The sight of ice in July stills a mind, raising a question I rarely address. What other wonders do I walk the surface of? A few yards higher, in temperate sunlight, blueberries ripen

31

in thick clusters. Commercial pickers pack the bounty in shavings of the selfsame ice, to ship to distant ports. They favor utility, inattentively gathering chips and burrs of some awesome monster for small private gain. Thus we play favorites among the everyday spirits.

The child is different. He lives still without disturbances of memory, in innocence of time remembered. His grip on himself is certain enough to allow the present to be announced and pass unrestrained. Ogres, trolls, and dwarfs march out of caves and past his unaverted glance. Only such courage do the chthonic monstrosities respect, for they do not wish to be devoured before their times. The same is true, only more so, of deeper powers of earth, who mothered time. The organism of a child has not learned to repel them. Nor has a thick outer crust confused perception and desire with a claustrophobic hideout for doubt.

In springtime a hickory sprouts buds to live through the winter following. So too a child who frolics in pure passion and who is stirred out of dreams to wonderment. Wonder, the most philosophic of feelings, is when time comes to a stop. In the arrest, a child, being both engulfed by and apart from time, ceases to be a spring lamb and is first touched by the quest of humanity. Who am I? What is my nature? For what end was I meant to be? To what powers am I beholden? Muddy spring waters soon overflow the banks. In floodtime, one must get a grip on oneself. In this time, the vow is born.

The vow is the grip made to do service in the realm of feeling. Being avowed, the vow is secret, in the sense that the child binds himself only unto himself. In a darkened bedroom, in a hiding place known only to him, he says with full passion, "I will be good," "I will never do that again," "I will obey." Or "I will get my revenge." The utterance is natural, like driving rain of mid-March, and works in ignorance of itself. A sluice cut here, a riverbed scoured there, ravines canceled, channels blocked or remade: Much of what we call "character" results from the force a child has called into being by solemn words.

Do not underrate the solemnity of childhood. No time is more solemn, more reasoned. Though he lacks syllogisms, the child applies logic to action in a direct, truthful manner—which proves we adults surpass his reason in one area alone: the lie. To lie and to break a vow are, to a child, deeds totally without redeeming value. To vow is a child's secret insofar as he understands his necessity. To break a vow (however trivial to adult eyes) is to break the vessel of his being. Strange silences, odd recalcitrances, bizarre avoidances in walking (step on a crack, break your mother's back), refusals to look or taste: These often are workings of an innocent vow. The extremes (punishment, disapproval, rejection) a child endures to honor a pledge demonstrate the mysterious force that binds him. It is stronger than any torment that can be inflicted on his will.

Aristotle calls habit "second nature." That makes it a set of clothes or a thatching to a basic structure. So habit enjoys a visibility the vow—the ridgepole of our nature—does not. Character displays the walk, dress, manner of speech, facial expression, posture, and gesture of a creature. The vow, by contrast, is secret, born in secret, as Earth in a dark cave bore her sons who would eventually topple time. A child feels injustice, indignity, and betrayal of trust. The child's will gives itself to an incantation that conveys a heat of moral consciousness. In that fire is forged an implement that is a weapon against time. This is the promise. The promise sealed by "I will" disappears from view in a mind for which burial is incubation. The germ grows strong and eternal by multiplying itself. A child governed by the seasons forgets, but the vow does not. It repeatedly brings forth new vows, raging against time, pricking the conscience of their guarantor.

Such are the hidden channels through which consciousness flows. For ourselves, children of our childhood, who among us has not come up against an invisible barrier, a hesitancy on the brink of action, across which we cannot move? The vow's prohibitive commandment cuts deeply into the bedrock of a person, impeding a search for self-knowledge until the spell is broken. This one cannot look his brother in the eye, another must speak in circumlocutions to elders, still another pushes herself to a breakdown. Exemplary vows continue to police response and uphold long-since-forgotten honor. They are stops placed on time while one is in the grip of immense strength. They are encoded themes in a melody of existence. They offer refuge for the need for integrity people do not love us for.

This explains a child's delight in hiding places. A hiding place is the vow remade into a home. Woe be to the boy or girl who divulges the secret. What place then is safe? But we must be clear. A child does not keep a hiding place to hide *from* others, but to discover again the hiddenness of things. She secrets herself to renew a pledge of being, to dream of fulfillment, and to return to what cannot be pledged—the source of all vows and collateral for a promised future. The back side of things, the darkened space in which illuminated images play, a child does not forget—until she forgets her vow. A primitive fear lives here, as well as awe and wonder. In fact, fear (which on the ladder of passions stands below anger) almost always suspects that the object has an unseen rear portion from which an ogre may erupt to threaten to our being. When a hiding place becomes an escape (the resort or weekend retreat), fear recedes from awareness, gripping vows at the roots. Then fear's ransom is higher. The fear we recognize demands less than the one we do not. When hideouts in trees and caves lie abandoned, vows cease their calm appeal and grow perilous.

Strangely, a child comes out of hiding in the den safe from sight. Heraclitus, who once mentioned that time is a child playing counters, knew the nature of childhood, for he notices how nature loves to hide. Those who value a mossy rock in the pine forest where they cannot be found know why. Reticence is put aside to deal with what vows set in motion—which also come out of hiding. Ali Baba knows the lesson well, since he overcomes two score of thieves to gain a hidden treasure. I wonder how remembrance of a sacred place is lost. One day my young son said to himself, "Someday you will understand," over and over again. Had he overheard someone else, or was it a self-admonishment? Did it intimate an endless process by which to come to the grace of knowledge? He was not discouraged by the lack, since it did not arise by loss or fall. "Someday" was a promise that granted equanimity. It set him face-to-face with his limits and the limitlessness of what was promised him to know, himself. This is the outlook of an everyday spirit who rolls rocks in front of cave doors. The same spirit recalls the password, *open sesame*. Boulder moves to one side, cave stands open, treasure is revealed. What could be simpler?

To promise to fill empty hands is a grave undertaking. But who can foreknow the gravity? This is Sindbad's strength: to end his poverty. Its fulfillment allows an endless retelling of his story. Empty hands are presents of angels' absence. *This* vow has a special weight for the one who takes it, for then an ordeal of existence has import. To become understanding, responsive, and knowing of a world that hides itself: That is to live with a sword dangled over one's neck. The sword would cut one off from meaning. Suffering would become mechanical, a sort of torture. Yet one moves with a fullness of that suspended moment.

Ali Baba could sleep in this position because he consorted with thieves. He could rest assured, knowing no value could be held on to. Emptiness might return at any time. Schoolmaster and merchant, tradesman and farmer, bookkeeper and nurse, however, expect consistency. Their logic is unaware of loss of the most precious thing. It agrees that what appears to be is the case. What has us look behind ourselves? Our suspicions being roused by a lie. How hard ordinary logic is for a child. We forget the great effort of a first "lie"—that lies against a naive avowal of understanding. What we learn is an art or artfulness. We catch on to how to steal from truth in order to catch a little sleep. We say: treasure waits, we will find the cave—only to maintain a semblance of order for now. Time moves on for a child, too, while understanding grows farther off, somehow less important. This is a despair of gravity. The same art, which is also a dissembling, is a cure. Tell a lie often enough, and its substance evaporates, leaving only marsh gas rising over a clear pool of conscience. One look, and time is devoured by the reflection. The waters are not seen again. The thing lost is oneself.

Yet the illusion gets a child—and ourselves—over a difficult moment. A glimpse of truth reveals the precarious matter of human reality. A moment before, the predicament of the swamp paralyzed us. Now the scene appears unthreatening. This small improvement has been wrought by the vow. Where has this vexing everyday spirit gone? To behold the space between lucid surface and noxious vapors is to welcome the vow.

As forger and counterfeit, the vow is poet of lies. Yet always, there is a yearning for truth—embellished but secure, artful but gentle. This yearning is of love, and love driveth out all fear. The vow thus prepares the world for the child, and the child for the world. A swamp is a secret place where schooling takes place. There, someday—someday I will understand—is barely within the shimmering light, a swift movement of goldfish, a swaying of bullrushes whose roots are invisible. The vow instructs. This is not utopia, it says. Everything looks set for play, but look! Monsters hide right below.

6

JACK FROST

Jack Frost is surely here. He bites the fingers and bites the toes. By day, his lacy pattern disappears from the window in the returning sun, yet he returns undaunted each night. A morning after his first arrival, children play fox and geese in whitened field grass. Magic has been at work. Stalks lose their resilience, apples gain a deeper grain, locusts suddenly quiet. For a farmer who reads signs pragmatically, the time is not for games but for filling the corn crib and mending the barn door. The life that is to be will continue inside only through husbanding of provisions. A farmer knows the value of reticence, if only not to boast about his readiness within earshot of a merciless nature. But to a child all is play, and the game, to capture the creature sly enough to live off another's foreknowledge.

A fox is no grasshopper whose payment for a midsummer's dance (Aesop tells) is winter starvation. A fox is adept at plundering the farmer's coops and pens for fowl. Now in deep snow, now in first mud, with slush making the circle, the chase is on—though a child (unlike a farmer) wants the fox's secret of cleverness, not his pelt. As a fox runs, first after geese then from them, so a child chases and is chased by a desire to catch what can outwit a farmer. It exhilarates. Breath grows hotter, face redder. And all the time, Jack Frost, the presiding spirit, looks on, for it is he (who is more clever, more adept at theft?) who is object of the romp.

Jack Frost, I hear, always wears a mask. At one end of his stay, the ghoulish pumpkin face of Halloween casts a candlelit smile across a

37

bare porch. At the other a fat Mardi Gras face grins lustily just before the long fast preceding spring rebirth. More than anything, more than a Paschal Lamb, a midsummer's sweet rose, or bearded barley of the harvest, Jack Frost brings the seasons to focus. What is a year? Emerald green, a piebald garden, and mists and mellow fruitfulness all pass, for a child, as a dream. Skin is bathed in sun that imperceptibly but regularly shifts above the playground. Like in the movement from minute to minute of an hour hand, no sharp difference stands out from one day to the next. One frosty nip at the nose changes that. A child wakes to a new lesson.

What is the teaching? It has nothing to do with time and a crime of infanticide that swallows whole a child's simple taste for reality. Now neglect of his mittens imparts what it means to act out of season: tears, heartache, and loneliness. For Jack Frost is a cruel and impartial spirit. His carnival merry-go-round cannot slow for dropped scarves, dislodged boots, displaced hats, or trophies dropped in his snowdrifts. The solace of understanding does not ease a painful inadvertence, for we are not dealing with a loss that can be erased. The pain is otherwise. It is pain of separation.

The year must move on, toward maple sap's rising, jonquils and forsythia, the planting of the potato eyes, and honeybees' swarming. An elemental clarity—cipher of bare trees against early dusk—is compromised by muddy waters. A rich profusion of the other quarters of the year quickly soothes the sting. A stark brick wall again sports ivy leaf, beautiful to behold. But before this happens, a primal feeling shows its face. One has felt that one does not belong.

The holy inhumanity of the seasons is repeated in Jack's mask. The mask also does not belong, and though taken off to reveal the face of a sibling, it is essentially an alien feel. "Put off that mask of burning gold/With emerald eyes" (Yeats). I have seen a young child shriek in terror at a paper bag placed over a friend's face. Even when the mother removed it, no amount of convincing proved to the child the matter of identity. That matter is simple for us who have buried fear of being out of season. Why not cherries at Christmas and ice in July?

For a child, however, the otherness of Jack, who loathes unwary sluggards, is cause for fear and trembling. The otherness is a continual risk. A child cannot, like a farmer, calculate the time of sowing and reaping and lead a life of relative security—though a farmer, like a child, lives with fear of late frost, wet growing season, storm at harvest time. The other's power lives in its arbitrary exercise. By a whim it

snows at apple blossom time. The crop is stunted. A mask similarly
takes pleasure in unexplained effects. It looks at you, and you develop
a rash, or some calamity befalls your mother. People still quake at the
evil eye, which is the other's eye through the peephole of a mask. The
value of the lesson is apparent to farmer and child. Woe to one who
does not mind the sharp tattoo of Jack's drum!

The pulse is a drum that beats to one's heartbeat. A teaching of
cycles and rhythms of nature touches us on the raw. Is this sensitive
nerve not the cause of superstition for a child? Refusing a goody, feign-
ing illness, not salting his food, eating left-handed: Quirks may be
prompted by an inward season of his day. The hardship of being "a
man for all seasons" is real. Jack may nip a desire in the bud or snow
another under just when the bloom is ready to be plucked. The world
is not happy with a man who is consistently responsive. His moral rigor
is all too apparent. It also is changeful, marching to a fickle drummer.
Thomas More, who had the love of Henry VIII, fell out of favor for
this reason and ended badly, in the tower. His martyrdom is one way to
escape death, for such a man escapes by keeping pace, never letting his
heart be bought by unseasonal fruits. No price is enough to pay for the
tears, heartache, and loneliness of falling out of step.

The truth is, time does not age us, the seasons do—or our heed-
lessness of them. In the country, one drives frost away with his saw and
axe; the years turn faces to leather. The city heats with coin and paper.
Faces become soft like dough. Philosophy is like a city dweller in how
it warms to cold abstractions. Abstractions prepare a thinker for death,
since they bear no seasonal life. They speak of eternity without regard
to tenses. A philosopher (like Socrates) grows old in ignorance, which
is a kind of self-knowing, not learning the corrected form of things
sudden frost teaches. The cold loosens one's grip enough to recognize
a face of unseasoned action that leers behind a carnival mask. It is oneself, too mindful to the present folly.

What do philosophers know of such impartiality? The yearly
cycle never affects their thought. So long as one's feet are warm, an
inclination toward timeless truth is not easily defeated. Legend has it
that Socrates went barefoot even in wintertime. In the midst of battle,
Alcibiades reports, Socrates stood thus, wrestling with these hoary
implications, refusing to give it up "till morning, and then at sunrise
he said his prayers to the sun and went away" (*Symposium* 220d). He
avoided images that swell the chest like a toad trying to outdo the ox.
Nakedness is not likely to forget the frosty whip that stings with its

reality. Socrates' courage is as great as that in taking on an angel. To imitate his act is simple. One need only to take off one's wraps and delight in the frigid blast that tests lofty plans. Such action contrasts with a farmer's practicality and returns us to a child's ardor. It meets the spirit of Jack Frost with an open heart.

Winter fields have been dry this year. Winterkill—milkweed, goldenrod, Queen Ann's lace, and, below, the yarrow—is an odd fruit, enduring yet fragile, brittle yet bending, harsh yet welcoming. A blanket of snow would change nothing essential so long as harvest remained unburied. The beauty of a January pasture works strangely on one. Green stalks whose life the frost has sucked belong to a dream; also, to the pithy wisdom of growing. Now the metaphor is stark and unyielding. So many hiding places stand revealed, a nest in boxwood, a bramble lair, a tangled currant bush. Things are returned to their being.

This explains why a cold still-life is disquieting. It tells of distance, entanglement, and overconcern. A perfumed garden offers an intoxicating air, and we breathe its forgetfulness in. The stalks that Jack kills are a mind's, for this is how it happens when conscience awakens. Dread of tears, heartache, and loneliness gives way to actual pain, which is lesser and more nourishing. Besides, a simple remedy is apparent. Put on your gloves and collect a bouquet of everlastings blanched by ice. Their unflinching resilience offers a new truth.

Many false springs pass before the real thing. A groundhog sees its shadow and burrows back into its underground home. Its is a primitive prediction, but winter extends until we warm to our own desires. For a child, it is different. He is moved to lie face up in late snow to create angels by a simple action of his arms and legs. Or to make a snowman or build a snow house. The mystery of substance that changes in his grip sustains him, though his gaze does not rest long in one place, lest the face behind the mask appear. The pulse of life beats its frenzied rhythm, and blood stays warm.

Our desires, however, show signs of venerable age. Detached from the seasons, they point beyond their fulfillment. Such knowledge does not belong to a friend of Jack Frost and is a single great advantage of being an unseasonal creature. I do not mean the pragmatics of waiting for the balm of a spring night to desire one's lover. Any night will do. Or any day, since if temperate climate changes no inner clock, desires respect no law of cycles. But without internal seasons, a hidden contradictoriness of desire comes out of hiding. Very much of our suffering can be traced to this fact. For a remedy, we cultivate choice by

reason—that can have a frostbite of its own. But reasoning by difference, genus and species (left by Aristotle the physician) are mere pallia-
tives. They create priorities to mask pain. An inevitable glimpse of contradiction brings with it new possibilities and new obligations. They
stare us down. They are like eyes of an owl in the dark woods, just
until spring truly breaks, with intoxication and desire.

A child fills with late-winter restlessness. A skim of mud tops the
frozen ground this Celtic new year but is not deep enough to sink
into. An appetite for pageantry has been whetted during a month-long
fast, but a north wind still brings rime each dawn to wake him from
dreams. In the stove, logs sing louder than the cardinal that beats back
wintry death. It is the season of maple icicles, for sap now rises. Animals stir from hibernation for first nourishment before again giving
themselves over to sleep. An old farmer may take his wife's molasses
and sulfur, mix of the hot and the sweet, to purge stagnated veins. The
moment is as delicate as ice rimming the brook's stones, so tempting
to pulverize under a child's boot. A frustrated stoppage reigns, as if
Jack were keeping a finger in the dike until the flood tide overwhelms
his waning power.

Creatures of stagnation are different from those of a rushing,
plunging creek. Though vision is dimmed by refusal, a duality of the
time—what is together with what is about to be—is nonetheless
apparent. The bittersweet ache of a yearning heart is about to be
replaced by vibrant spring love. But is it supplanted or, like deep sleep
is by the dream, only obscured? A child accepts a world of levels,
regardless of his terror of hidden depths, dark woods, eyes behind the
mask. He is impelled past painful contradictions, into a full flowering
of vernal desire before late snowfalls. No amount of warning keeps a
coat on him in the last days. Adult life is different. We are caught on
the cusp of conflict because of world leveling. Reality has width and
extent but really no depth nor breadth. Our tears fall on flat terrain.
Falling, they remind us of a new dimension suffering reveals. This is
Jack Frost's final work.

Jack releases us from the loneliness we feel when cut off from the
source of seasonal change, this quixotic everyday spirit. He recalls a life
behind the ever-changing mask as well as the changelessness of that
life. Reminded of what abides, we lose the anxiety of time. Winter
passes, the robins return. Look! Oniongrass sprouts! Jack releases us
finally to the joy of a new spring.

7

DAFFODILS

They arrive already knowing the lay of the land. They are gypsies, some in rags, some in jags, some in velvet gowns. I have seen dogs bark at them. They make a rhapsody, first in simple reed, then in showy trumpet. The Death that never dies is dead. Long live the spring! Daffodils have returned.

Look at a jonquil. A simple thick stalk does its job unobtrusively. It throws a flamboyant bloom up to rival the diffident April sun. The head is all show, frilly collar, open at the throat, multiple rays for each compass point, earthly and celestial. A solar apostrophe, nothing is held back. But as with all show, a jonquil is weak scented, barren, and short-lived. It is an advent. Soon the full-dress rehearsal of spring begins. But before, the herald, all gauded up, steals the stage. He begins: We have fasted and been penitent. Now we feast on winter's dead body. Let us begin....

This is a prayer also. For even songbirds maintain their silence above on bare limbs. If earth could speak through cracks and ruptures created by a jonquil's stalks, it would be a reveille.

I am not thinking of annunciation. Woods are magical, fields the farmer's, and a violence of awakening merely a dispelled lullaby. A child opens her eyes, and the world is green again. No interval leaves its impression for questioning. Hence no hard thought is needed to dispel mists of suffering—wiles of the dream. To those eyes, a daffodil is excess, exuberance, embellishment. Nature is not so severe as to pretend austerity as sun warms skin. She lifts her skirt. A child lifts her shirt

43

above the belly. A fecund center is exposed. The act announces present purpose. No future awaits its turn.

But although full, the present is not fertile. The time is not yet for procreation. The show is all barrenness. What business is more barren than an orgy? Excess is enjoyed for its own sake, not for any other. Accidents are stripped from a body, revealing lust for essence. The essential lust, hidden away under wool wraps and made to serve other spirits, now spurts forth. It will serve only one master, itself. When there were gods, one spoke more delicately, of "Pan," "Dionysus," or "Bacchus." But early spring wine and song of the daffodil are more direct. Dispense your seed. Join the primal One whose lewd laughter wipes memory clean. Unbend your pleasure this moment. The labor of insemination can wait, as well as the harder work of bearing fruit. Spend—the earth is poor. Together we will work its transformation. So sings this everyday spirit.

Few resist the trickery of the daffodil. Dawn is chilling, and dusk early, but danger of night seems endless. Danger? Disrobement, loss of propriety, uncivil conduct, seductive speech, animal cries. An oblivion of this waking sleep is only a blink from the lullaby. An orgiastic dithyramb quickly follows the dreamless state as need arouses resourcefulness. "Of restless nights in one-night cheap hotels" (T. S. Eliot). Sleeping Beauty stirs, wakened by a kiss. She discovers her sleep, her hunger, and her prince all at once. In a first blink, her virginity is lost. This unwariness is trickery itself, double trickery. Such is wisdom of the bloom without a seed.

A first trick is the lesser. Nature allows us lust—which is free and single minded—in order to exact her payment—to multiply exceedingly. We must leave another in our place. Only later do we discover the cost of enticement. A second is the greater. Nature grants us excess in order to free us of all cravings. How could a creature of desire ever desire to be desireless? We glimpse that the palace of wisdom, as Blake puts it, lies just beyond the way of excess. That realization flowers at a height of craving, before petals grow limp with heat and drop, before the trumpet's mouth pouts cloyingly, before sweetness leaves. It validates the daffodil's excess and values it higher than stoicism—which winter and philosophy alike share. Which explains why a child would rather gather daffodils than gather syllogisms.

But the daffodil does not appeal to everyone. What is the abandon we fear to meet? It is a pauper's bloom as well as a child's. Charities sell them to raise mission money. The rich and the self-made overlook them for the more devout asphodel. Even Sindbad does this, for his way to gold dictates an austere grip on things and values labor as salvation. A gushing love fills no coffers. It empties a hero's tensed muscle, leaving the shell porous, open to invitation or invasion. It assaults boldness and reticence alike. Laughter does the same thing, breaking form and definition and spilling out the stuff of contradiction—which brings us to the revel.

A revel is always attended by laughter. An orgiastic laugh escapes our categories. It is neither mad nor intoxicated nor savage nor beastial. Yet it throws itself out of joint, joining heaven to earth's body by means of an unflowered spear, an unfurled jonquil. Contradiction means suffering, clash of lance against lance. The laughing daffodil shoots spikes that do not cross (save in the wind.) Hence, the ego is pricked painlessly. Its dried scum, resembling the flower's thin outer sheath, makes barely a blemish on the primal countenance. Almost nothing is added to the indissoluble One. This fact has always been fertile ground for prophets. Though the daffodil's body rises reborn from a debris of past life, this does not symbolize resurrection. This is another difficult fact. Prophets would never think of garlanding the savior with daffodils. Daffodils bloom is too much of the body and droop too quickly toward its rising pleasure.

A child (who is a farmer) knows the spirit of digging. There is a mystery of the bulbous root. She is not yet a reticent pragmatist whose knowledge is of flowers and consequences. "By the fruits, not the roots" is a motto .of sorts. It denotes a glance heavenward, a beatific pose that leaves one to trip over gnarled protuberances jutting underfoot. A child would never miss them on her life. Earth's softened shell calls. Unknown things lie buried beneath. Secret movements give rise to the whole visible world. An act of exertion exposes hidden contents, tunnels of worms and grubs, germinating pods, hairlets of trees and shrubs, cold dark pebbles. This act points to discovery, which is a heaven itself.

A thinker is wary of appearances. He seizes a shovel and breaks through the surface. Plato's hyperbole is to say that surface is deceitful. It is the place of illusion and mirage. On a hot summer day, macadam is this way, a brilliant play of heat shadow. I am not often taken in, though when I am, the road becomes a stage for sudden appearances, a djinn, a rare bird, a sea monster—Sindbad's place. A philosopher asks which is mirage, road or dragon. He warns that reality is made of other stuff, less friable and more durable than either. His is a mind of analogy. "Do you think that these men would have seen anything of themselves or of one another except the shadows cast from the fire on the wall of the cave that fronted them?" Plato asks. (*Republic* 7.515c). The metaphor penetrates a casual acquaintance with the world. What appears on the cave's surface is seeming reality. What does its unreality depend on? A shovel.

One digs. Light follows. The surface is only a temporary stopping place. Root is exposed, no longer dark. The rule of light is extended downward. A new order of knowledge results. In a final exclamation, Plato declares that light itself is the shadow of God. Light too must be turned over with a spade and its innards let spill, if we ever are to face directly heaven's countenance. Such a mind is always busy. For as blade cuts into soil, fresh surface quickly stales. Always to dig deeper until one reaches the light that is shadow: This is a philosopher's life. Which explains why the philosopher Hume had to push aside his spade in order to enjoy backgammon. Happiness is deferred in favor of equipoise.

A philosopher eschews excess. It is ill health itself, Aristotle the physician declares. Temperance—which seeks the golden mean by skirting extravagances and austerities—is a way of hygiene. To drop a shovel (mind's invention) and scoop with the hands: The act becomes an end in itself. A child has no real hope of reaching China, where Confucius saw particulars as things in themselves. Muck is pleasure enough. It is flesh on flesh, orgiastically pungent. Rub the hands together joyfully. In this simple act of laving, the poem is born. Strangely, in mood it is an idyll.

A poet is a person of justice. How else to take things as they come, without seeking buried treasure? This is how to justify the ways of God to man, the poet says: "what in me is dark/Illumine, what is low raise and support" (Milton). His way of meting out judgment (meter, in the literal sense) is makeshift. Earth provides matter, heaven form, and a poet affirms a preestablished harmony. Since the poem flits daimonically between the two realms, its voice is strange and harsh. It is not of the gods—who thunder and hail and inveigh from the heights—still less of farmer, woodcutter, or bushman, who croaks commands to the oxen.

The gods love or fear the poem, depending on whether it teaches reverence for them. The ancients saw it as a derivation from the celestial music of Hermes. This is shortsighted, since the divine guide traded his lyre to Apollo, who had a niggardly spirit toward humanity.

Another, more important reason is that the poem carries the voice of a seeker. To search, as was said, is an occupation foreign to the gods. One who seeks one's self moves within a paradox of incompleteness. One is not fully who one thinks one is, yet who else could one be? The fervor and anguish of the question disturbs an earthly political state. If its citizenry listen to the poet and give themselves wholeheartedly to a search for being, instability, ineptitude, and insurrection would result. The "leviathan," as Hobbes called political society, would be in a shambles. For this reason, Plato vehemently excludes all poets from the republic. This is a misfortune for all. For justice is a poet's calling, and he reckons words he crafts on the balancing pans of actuality. With the grimy hands of a child, he fashions his expressions willy-nilly from the freshly covered soil of his experience. What could be more just than voicing this selfsame actuality? What pleasure does child (and poet) find with the slime? One needs to dig a little to come to the question. The senses certainly are fed, tactilely, visually, and viscerally. Some argue in favor of a titillation of sex drive, and I would not deny that good, viscous mud may trigger memories of birthing, caverns, and the Earth Mother. An imperative of discovery, however, arises from another source. The child (poet) is on a quest to see nature. He is the primordial scientist. An amorphous clot of earth is, to his touch, the vehicle of great knowledge. It must be prodded, poked, jabbed, stabbed, and shaped until it yields its inherent form, form itself. The form, a mound or pie or sonnet, announces itself in an enduring contact between his hands and the substance.

The child or poet, moreover, is not creator of form but its witness. His act, of supreme joy, is an observation of laws of nature. We must be clear here that observing requires that no separation exist between the event and the attention. Distance means death, a deadening of a vital participation in what takes place. Hence, a child's bliss and the reason for tending daffodils is discovery of one's own nature. That is what shines darkly from just inside the surface of one's cup of muddy water.

Daffodils are coming! They are manifest. Their spikes have risen from their dull, bulbous palace (a rhizome, really), and their crowns announce appearance, the show, the look, and what seems to be. Winter had depth, reality, being, but spring is becoming! It does away with all that solemnity. What really has arisen—the orgy, or what it precedes? Symposiasts have gathered until our times to pursue this question. Some say quickened desire has a taste of immortal life itself. At least in an afterglow, one is compelled to speak of immortal things, truth and beauty. That is the way that is still beholden to the gods, who deify the libido and propagate its appetite without end. Even a child knows mud will dry, cake the fingers, and require cleansing before one goes on with other things. Mud is a season one seeks out. But then, one is done with it. What was it for? While the sun comes to prepare a bed for more enduring blooms, spike is capped by the flower itself. Its knowledge, quiet, self-contained, serene, is a vantage point of what lies beyond childhood and poetry. In another age, from another place, the Buddha watched the lotus blossom also rise from a muddy bottom. In response to that vision, he proclaimed a different way to immortality, through a practice of nondesire. Whether new or not, the face he saw watching him from the yellow throat was both unknown and familiar. In the fresh bloom, he saw his Self.

PART TWO

EUMAEUS

8

HOUSEGUESTS

We, the human species, seek shelter. Cave, hollow tree trunk, fallen rock slide, vine-matted jungle lean-to: These were trial habitats. They gave way to tent, teepee, and thatched-roof hut. Happenstance made room for will as we began to occupy shelters differently. As to when we become householders and home dwellers, the question demands an indirect approach. Socrates warns that a philosopher's work takes hold only outside the human dwelling. A house is no place for philosophy, the way its concerns preempt a mind. In a house, each thing assumes definition and refuses to allow idle hands. Always, some thing needs fixing.

House and its dweller are upright. Not that the countryside is without disguises (which is fodder for speculation). A farmer who knows the pitfall of reading a sun-filled September day at face value has cultivated an elaborate fatalism. I mean that uninhabited nature shows a difference between essence and accident, or (returning to Socrates) need and necessity. Having a roof over our heads, walls to keep out wild beasts, and fire under the pot, we discover a householder's first need—to take in guests.

The uncanny nature of human habitation is stranger than the peculiar trait of keeping pets of other species in our homes. The uncanniness is real. It is the indeterminate, the random, the unsecured, the risk-laden, the devil wind that tips in windows and topples the chimney pot. No sooner is the structure sealed against the elements than we open the door to an uninvited guest. Let in Chance herself.

51

Cap the roof with a symbolic tree, and warm the fire with a guest's presence. What better way to keep hounds of necessity at bay than to remind heaven of the need to host? Necessity lives not outside a house, but in habit born of the hearth itself. Habitation *is* habit—and we its prisoner—until we allow entry to a human element. Welcome the guest! Her spirit unsettles a head nodding toward dreams before an afternoon fire. Laws of hospitality permit no easy sleep.

Again I jump ahead of the story. Who is the binding spirit of house and hearth? Who sweeps the dust, repairs the roof, and empties ashes from the stove? Who turns lights up in the evening and off before bed? Have we ever seen the spirited being who cooks, shovels snow from a walk, opens a window for the west wind, or collects dried everlastings for the herbal? Does she pass too closely to be noticed? At home, where we return to ourselves, we drink of the waters of Lethe. The act is prior to, but not different from, the dreaming that distracts from true sleep. In a dream, we grow restive and dispirited. Pettiness becomes the mien. Things out of place are annoying, while chores command attention: dirty windows, dull knives, and filled ashtrays. We rail against our lot as servants to an unknown master. At home, we forget to welcome ourselves in. Who then is missing?

How refreshing to read of Eumaeus, who kept house in a rude swineherd's hut, ever mindful of his master's absence. Against hope, he hopes for Odysseus's return, to set things again to order. Meanwhile, he makes notable improvements in the homestead, high walls "of quarried stone" around the yard, a stockade of oak "taken from the dark heart of the logs," a hedge of wild pear. No dust gathers on his heels. His largesse increases in the desert of his heart. That day will come when he will throw open the doors of the house once again....

Listen to Eumaeus as he greets the raggedy tramp at his gate: "My conscience would not let me turn away a stranger in a worse state even than yourself, for strangers and beggars all come in Zeus's name, and a gift from folk like us is none the less welcome for being small." It is his lord he greets. For this reason in holier times, hospitality was universal sacred law. To turn away a guest or to defile his company was an open invitation to a lightning bolt from above. But risk is involved in all dealings with higher natures. The one who comes to dinner might be a burgler or spy or plain parasite. Is there some special protection? Eumaeus has the householder's amulet. Humility lets his character be revealed by hosting an unknown presence. He knows why the house is kept.

Bourgeois possession makes no one a householder. Instead, it crams a house with trinkets. A farmer is closer to keeping his house than a city dweller, not because he owns less stuff, but because he can put it outside in a barn or shed. Farm things are thus more expendable, more readily replaced. Once one is a burgher, desire fills a house with objects. Dreams that disturb nocturnal renewal are of acquisition. To host and to have: These acts have a common home, which is in the grasp of one's hand. But they move opposite one another, as opposite as a clenched fist is to a gently guiding pressure at one's elbow. Things lose their value to humankind when they cease being gifts and become articles on account. Before, their comings and goings were no part of human power. A burgher, however, defines his estate by the ledger sheet. Objects entered must be kept until replaced, repaired, or disposed of. The chore is a never-ending busyness.

Burgher, city dweller, and farmer have exchanged need for necessity. All economies follow suit. Necessaries obey a logic of replacement. If one's sandal is lost, a boot or shoe will do. If one's foot is gone, a crutch will suffice. If a most desired thing is unavailable, a next best will be fine. The path diverges from that of true desires. In the folktale, a poor farmer does not know how to wish for anything real. Rescuing a djinn, he is granted a boon of three wishes. Anything is his that his heart desires. But to his heart he does not listen. Hunger has him wish for a plate of sausage. His wife ires him, and anger has him wish her beaten with the sausage. When she begs mercy, repentance uses the last wish to restore her to health. Three wishes gone, and no thing gained. We mimic the farmer with his conservative economy of ploughing fields the way his father and his father's father did before him. No thing new is wished for. A call of need within evokes no response. Our house imprisons us.

A duality arises from deep in our nature. The word *host* itself reflects the contradiction in its ambiguity. We equally host gods and microbes. Human death can come from higher life as well as lower. The entity that comes into my home: What really is foreknown? It could be Elijah or my worst enemy done up as Elijah. Perfect humility—of Eumaeus—cuts like a sword through disguise.

Take the humble couple of Ovid's *Metamorphoses*, Baucis and Philemon. A pair of ruffians appear one stormy night at their front door. The hut is rude, their cupboard poor, only a single bowl of tallow gutters in the wind. But the hosting spirit is strong upon them. No shame do they feel for their table, their belongings, or their condition, which is an inner plenitude. Their only need is to obey an impulse to host. The dirt floor is hard but clean, and by the hearth is a simple granite shrine. The guests of dubious character sit at a rough table and give no sign. Philemon, the good woman, begins to pour from a pitcher of goat's milk, for no other libation is available. Imagine her astonishment when cups fill with wine, and the table becomes heavy with meats "and other dainties." The guests are no men but gods. Zeus and Hermes are testing (as Joseph and Mary would in another age) the law of hospitality. For receiving the strangers, Baucis and his wife reap rich reward.

The other side of the word *host* joins giver and recipient as twin snakes coiled around a common rod. Hermes' caduceus shows an image of unity in opposition. In reality, separate existences of guest and host are not what they seem to be. What binds them together? A home in which one serves and the other is served. The home encloses the opposing forces, places them in balance, and allows them together to serve one another—and perhaps a higher purpose.

A guest is one whose sharp eye disentangles accidental clutter from essential stuff. A house is designed to be a receptacle, a storeroom, a depository for castoffs, things out-of-season, articles of sentimental value, mementos, baubles, anything that takes up space. Such are attracted to a house by a law of conservation and begin to occupy attics, basements, and spare rooms like a conquering army. Life in a house piles up atop a vast archeological dig, if we ever dig down. A guest performs such a valued function. Experience her discerning eye. Things are cleaved of private associations and special history. Relics are seen for what they are. A true guest has come in from the road and knows that most is discardable if only an honest heart is willing.

A guest moves us closer to the ground. She disciplines a preoccupied self, allows us to suffer riches or poverty, and enters with news of the outside. She has traveled from afar. She has been long along the way. She bears witness to a forgotten world. News from abroad, travelers' accounts, logs, and war stories break the daily round of chores and renew a spirit of repetition. The world is always the New World. Its call may not constrain us to trek across the sea. But discovery is of a new mind. We discover as hosts that we are *keepers* of the home. Without the caduceus, the world axis, the twin halves of creation—outside and in—would fly apart.

A home is meant for interchange of host and guest over a good meal and a glass of wine while a storm wind whips up the trees. Without salutory conversation, the land remains mute. Between nomad and hermit, very little passes. A home is a true universal in Aristotle's sense, a cauldron in which particular things inhere, melt down, and become alloyed—to forge new things.

"Come in. Do let me take your coat." Some such expression is a part of a host's ritual greeting. The words initiate one into the role of host. They are welcoming, as I said, but also serve another function. Host takes guest's wraps and makes her at home. That is, he undresses the guest, takes the disguise with the help of which a guest appears in public, and returns a guest to her natural state. There is relief, nervousness ("Will I be accepted thus?"), and sudden intimacy of the guest. If a host participates, he strangely find himself also being undressed.

To stand fully clothed before another who has been unveiled is an act of domination, not hospitality. An act of entry has a counterpart in the sexual act. Lover undresses his beloved and admires her naked form. For himself not to undress is to leave the act without possibility of consummation. Sexual union, moreover, depends on dissolving a difference of outside and inside. Initially, lover comes from the outside into his beloved. Thereafter, they dwell together without boundaries in the moment. Intimate encounter is the center of hospitality, for time present exists by the hearth of eternity.

In common parlance, guest and host have a business they need to get down to. They have exchanged niceties, formulas of passage. They have broken bread together, sipped wine after toasting the gods of the table and bedside. Now they sit by a fire, earnestly attending each other. The host is strangely silent. What needs to be said? The host listens, waiting. He has not yet heard what completes an exchange—that is to say, what allows him and his guest to exchange places. He, like Atlas, has borne his duty without complaint, even with a joy. He now feels a need to be relieved. In the den, every sound is muted. As the host waits, his hope fades.

What needs to be expressed between guest and host? One is reminded of the Grail legend, of the first encounter between Parsifal and the Maimed King. The kingly host suffers his wound in despair while famine and pestilence overtake his kingdom. He knows his cure is to come through an unexpected guest, but his marvelous castle is not easily found. When Parsifal rides up, a red knight on a white horse, the king puts on his best display of hospitality. No riches are spared. At a sumptuous banquet, the entertainment suddenly falls mute. All eyes turn toward Parsifal expectantly. But no word arises, for he is cut off from his heart. The king suffers in silence. Once again, his kingdom is the wasteland—all for want of a word.

What is missing in the encounter? The story tells of three little words, "What ails thee?" In our way, we would ask, "How *are* you?" A royal silence awaits the question of questions, the question of how one suffers one's existence. What are your wounds? How did you come by them? In what way are you looking for a cure? What, if anything, would help? The question is unremittingly personal. It is the only real question asked of a person.

"How are you?" What the king's answer is—"Fine," "All right," "Not so well"—is immaterial. The guest's role, I mentioned, is to distinguish essential from accidental, gold from dross. What state a host suffers or enjoys falls on the side of accident. The essential matter is to be reminded of the self whose state it is, of the forgotten stranger. The king and his subjects languish until the reminder is delivered. A host is not himself until a guest arrives on his quest. Nor are we ourselves.

Hospitality is a confrontation of the two that are one. Which leaves us with the matter of a philosopher. Socrates, we know, led a public existence. He never took in guests, never engaged in philosophy at home, but in the *agora*, marketplace, or gynmasium. He was never host. Yet he was hosted, often and by many in prominence, but only once was his deficiency called on him. It was Diotima who told him, "I don't know how you can hope to master the philosophy of Love, if *that's* too much for you to understand" (*Symposium* 207c). This gadfly of souls, this corruptor of youth, was a fitting martyr for philosophy. By abjuring the human role as host, his search could have no end. One question followed another with no relief for the wound. They consume me, he once declared, but I cannot stop myself. That is true. No one is in a position to help himself. The Maimed King awaiting the royal guest knows his helpless condition. But no one ever came into Socrates' dwelling place to ask, "What ails thee?" Consequently, his relentless figure lives, moving from court steps to public forum, even to the city walls, never stopping, always asking, never waiting to be asked.

9

KEYS

At dusk, listen. The tread of boots along a stone path comes to a stop, with the jingle of a keychain. The fall of a tumbler, the turn of a latch, the opening of a door. The householder has returned.

The key is a small thing, really. In earlier times, it was no more than an unadorned rod or shaft—an extension of a finger. But its power is great. The key is spirit of place. It is preserver, keeping things unmixed, stoppered either in or out. It is liberator, unlocking a mystery of confinement, letting things again intermingle. To every place, door or no, there is a key. For the key is above all its overseer—its steward. We should also add that the key can be destroyer of the place. When the key is lost, the place is forgotten, and things pass from the human realm into their home in higher or lower spheres. Which is why a householder guards his keys so carefully. His place is preeminently here on earth, and he wishes to enjoy it as he is.

Not everyone has keys to jangle. Walk down a busy street. A good ear (on a quiet day) is enough to pick out nomads and pilgrims from householders, or from office managers who keep house away from home. Larger keyrings belong to hired custodians of place, guards, doormen, superintendents, cleaning personnel. The sound of multiple keys bespeaks an absenteeism that afflicts the time. Call it the "proxy principle." It entitles appointed others to take on duties of our place, a thought that thinly disguises a sense of our dispensability. The thought is not new. When we examine tombs of ancient royalty, kings appointed stand-ins for their mortal selves. Whole families were

57

interred along with the dead emperor for this reason. True household-ers, by contrast, never pay for the services of someone to mind the keys. Who can lift from his shoulders the weight of keeping that place? His Herculean muscles support an upright morality. His heartfelt adherence to it keeps earth in its orbit beneath the fixed stars and above the primeval slime.

Nomad and pilgrim, by contrast, have abjured keys altogether. The latter gives up possessions cold in order to become unto the lilies in the field. The former gives up a single place in favor of mobility, "among all the walking people" (Rilke)—but does not relinquish pos-sessiveness (as the gypsy shows). A nomad's strategy is to outrun forces that would overwhelm him. He believes the foot is fleeter than the thief. Only wind and storm clouds are capable of stealing into his stronghold and removing an article of treasure. Some say he is there-fore more holy than a householder, since he does nothing to hinder the onrush of elements. His primitive freedom excites a poet who like-wise strives after fluidity—in his flight from chaos. But poet as well as worshiper of nomadics must acknowledge that holiness has more to do with a knowing attitude than with a style of life. Socrates suggests holi-ness is "a science of sacrifice and prayer" (*Euthyphro* 14e). Otherwise, keeping a house would be an act of impiety.

A place of dwelling has a key with which it can be opened or closed at will. This signifies an important fact about the keybearer, the householder's condition, our own. Our humanity, we saw, must be let in. As it is, we remain unfinished creatures. Put another way, a "some-thing" has to be unlocked in order to free our humanity, to free us to ourselves. Though we may search for it, this something has not yet been found. Until it is, and we become more available to what is secreted under lock and key, we remain lost to ourselves.

More particularly, palace dweller and tabernacle dweller alike have noticed that a most intimate dwelling place lies within the skin we call our own. Our body shelters us. We proceed tortoise-like through life, soft, vulnerable parts protected by a shell from invading forces without. But this fact comprises another part of the question that we are. If our flesh is no more than shell, it cannot be opened save by vio-lence. Because no provision has been made for a key, force must do what intelligence cannot. But if there really is a key to our bodily dwelling place, then it is more than husk or rusk or pod. It is a coating to the seed itself. Or like a creature of the sea, we can lighten or leaden this body by a peculiar act of will—once we surrender self-will. The act is nothing other than respect of the body for what it is.

The key belongs, I have said, to a steward. The lord of the place has absolute discretion as to who may enter, even unto prophecy. Odysseus in disguise avows to Eumaeus, "I swear now by Zeus before all other gods, and by the board of hospitality, and by the good Odysseus's hearth which I am approaching that everything will happen as I say." An awareness imbues the key with power. By the law of replacement that operates in the realm, keys become themselves bearers of power. Keys unlock not only doors, chests, boxes, and drawers (a horizontal door)—but also any secret whatsoever. Since a symbol is a secret until someone says what it symbolizes, all symbols require keys for their understanding. Maps and diagrams, codes and tables need keys to be read. To Plato, all knowledge is representative of reality. Knowing means holding the key to a symbol's truth. Which is to say, to the place where truth resides.

In modern, democratic times, a notion of secret knowledge is out of favor. This is a triumph of egalitarian over elitist, vulgarian over esoteric, cosmopolite over farmer, and businessperson over householder. Knowledge is as freely available as the air; one needs only to breathe it in. Little industry is needed to gather it. A cunning quest for a key to understanding is a thing of the past. Descartes helped perpetrate the new metaphor for seeking knowledge—he called for a lever rather than a key. The revision has tremendous import. Modernity can be dated from it. An image of brute, muscular exertion (Locke's notion of labor) replaces a wayfaring resourcefulness. We pry our way into a secret storehouse, wrecking doors as we go. No need to search out keyholder, hierophant, or teacher. As further proof of democracy, all able-bodied workers have the capability of wielding a crowbar. Why bother trying to unlock secrets when the hinges are sprung and the treasure room is waiting?

A queasiness about the superabundant store of knowledge can be traced to the new metaphor. A lever joins human ingenuity with animal strength. But without a key, we cannot tell knowledge from a dream. The glitter may be gold or our phantasy of great wealth. Where is the power of discretion? The key to knowing which is gold is consulting a sample. We need to be able to open to a truthfulness of the present situation. That which shines forth has an immutable face.

Descartes, who meditates on the question, locates the power otherwise, in thought. The approach seems odd for one who advocates physical leverage, but his choice discloses a deep confusion in will. He has difficulty telling dreams from actuality. This is because we both will and do not will the dream. We are cast in a dual role of dream hero and dreamer. We partake of a drama that we invisibly author. Truthfulness is strictly limited, since we lack a higher authority. A lever permits us to ignore limits and bully our way to judgment.

The juxtaposition of the lever and reason haunts our dwelling at home. Though by habit a homebody, Kant inherits this Cartesian coupling. He feels knowledge of any object remains on the subjective side. Although he says nothing on the matter, time and space (great abstractions!) become warp and woof of the dream fabric. There are strands or categories of thought that make up the dream of phenomena, *maya*. Of these, we dreamers have insider information. This constitutes our leverage. The design is the object, subjectivized. Of the real thing, however, everything remains unknowable. A model of the tapestry is never included in the design. Nor is a church bell that inspires a dream of a Sunday morning baptism included in the dream. Its unknowability lies in the fact it is beyond place. Being beyond place, it lacks a key. No key will ever unlock it for us. No everyday spirit will ever welcome us in. For Descartes and his followers, we will always be strangers in our house.

We may feel disquieted by an account that overlooks keys. To return to Kant, he reveals his intentions along this direction. The antinomies say as much. An antinomy proves both a position and its contradictory—which gives no key to the dilemma of whether time existed before time or if the soul is immortal. Yet antinomies are strangely reassuring. We rest easier when knowledge is kept behind a locked door. This stems from two different facts. First, as one's mind overbrims, one grows forgetful of daily realities. They do not, however, forget us, as barked shins, mangled fingers, bruised knees, and bummed toes say. Our need is to dwell in a place where crown jewels are under lock and key. Otherwise they might get misplaced. Unretrievable knowledge serves the purpose.

Second, abundance such as a mind has makes us feel cheap. Worth resides in a truly hard-won thing. When a triumph costs nothing, its value is the same. This situation marks a new poverty that afflicts the age of mass production, rapid transit, and fast food. Illusory riches cut us off from hidden treasure that may be gained (if at all) only at great expense. Again, an antinomy locks away what is beyond ordinary value. The key, our guiding spirit in matters of safekeeping, preserves knowledge and keeps it pure.

Some feel we retain a deep ambivalence toward householding,

dwelling in our place in the world. Has a householder abandoned the search or found a new vehicle for it? Is his place stagnant or at equipoise? The same ambivalence surrounds the keys he carries. How to understand the contention? Some have it that the key (signifying hidden valuables) invites danger. The ancients, for instance, knew Hermes as god both of keys and of thieves. If no thing were kept locked away, no one would be occupied in theft. The thought itself reflects an original ambivalence. The key does not create concealment but only capitalizes on it. Any place on earth both hides and reveals what is there. That is a condition of being under, but not in, heaven.

Pandora's story carries the same double message. Pandora ("all-giving"), it will be remembered, was as foolish and empty-headed a woman as she was beautiful. She came across a locked chest in which Prometheus had imprisoned all the Spites: old age, sickness, insanity, vice, and passion. The key lay beside it. With a deft twist of her wrist, she liberated all the beauties. Even that one, hope. We who are inheritors of her folly have also inherited a question: Would it have been better if hope had been kept under lock and key rather than freed? Is hope delusive? Now turn the question around toward a householder. Is the act of keeping itself what deludes us? For from the keeping arise ideas of permanence, sameness, and immutability. Thus the spirit of place—the key—tempts a householder. By its misuse he can lock himself away from change.

10

THE KITCHEN FIRE

Fire was the greatest of human discoveries. Long before it, ice and snow were the primeval condition. Then, humans did not seek refuge from a dream of infancy but reveled in it. In the golden age of lullaby, heaven and earth were separated by a mere breath. A child opening her eyes did not end the dream but embellished it with dream perceptions of the world. Under a blanket of snow, people banded together for warmth, in clans, tribes, families, and nations. The many were one. No essential difference wrested a single dreamer from the others. The "we" was synonymous with a "them." No verbs were declined, since each was at once subject, object, possessor, donor, and location.

Group consciousness extended a racial dream memory far backward, before birth. It contained heavenly beings as well as terrestrial ones. Angels walked among humans and participated equally in waking activities and dreams. The primordial word *I* was not yet known.

The momentous advent of fire changed all that. Our individuality was born of combustion. In ancient legends, the earth-power Prometheus stole fire from the gods and presented the theft to humans. (Who hasn't been a little Prometheus, stealing matches from the drawer beside the stove?) His punishment was excessive since he had disturbed a somnolent nature. Divinity has an interest in keeping us sleepers. Unaware of combustion, we remain ignorant of a fire of self. An unknowing servant is a profitable one. As automatons we serve sleeping nature and remain asleep to other possibilities—whatever the heavenly

63

intent is, "the floods of origin flowing within" (Rilke). Theft—of heat and transformation—opens a new place in a created and uncreated universe. Human beings learn of solitude; before, being alone, away from communal warmth, meant death by ice. Knowing solitude, they feel a flame that fired their unique nature, hitherto a frozen potency, from earth's clay. Growing warmer, they come to love and desire and seek immortality with a thinking heart.

A spark from a tinderbox plus kindling gives birth to fire. If we now turn back to Plato's gentle fable, need burns "with singeless flames" in one's viscera, stating its silent demand. Cold, dry, impoverished faggots of the soul, one's unignited wishes, provide fuel. Suddenly, spontaneously, there is combustion. It may seem that both fire and love arise solely by parthenogenesis, that they breed only from live embers of themselves. But as Plato describes, our poverty accepts an inseminating seed of our neediness, is consumed by a moment of passion, and brings a relating force forth into the world. Love and fire, fire and love. "Love is but a fire that is to be transmitted. Fire is but a love whose secret is to be detected" (Bachelard). Fire, force of relationship, belongs to no one party, for it itself transforms both. Inasmuch as it is a messenger—communicating an absence with a need to replenish—it is spirit or daimon. It flits back and forth between disparate realms, uniting them in their differences. It is hinge, joint, and yoke. It is change itself.

In pattern, color, intensity, warmth, and sound, fire is ceaseless, shifting movement. Hence fireplace or campfire performs a special function when we are young. Is there anything more enjoyable to watch? In its face, a world's preoccupations give way, through successive layers of reverie, association, and dream, to the storehouse empty of all imagery. Thus the flickering flame's power brings stillness. Watching, a child naturally assumes a posture. This posture is thought. Thought is born from fire.

Being Promethean and erotic, fire (among all phenomena of the house) embraces opposing values, good and bad, divine and satanic, useful and destructive. It lights the way to heaven. It burns a soul in hell. It thaws an embittered heart and disrupts peace of mind. The world ends catastrophically with fire. The day ends joyfully with fire. It is apocalypse and it is cookery.

For a householder, the last aspect needs a special treatment. In the house, fire occupies a unique physical place. At a center where fire is, is the kitchen. It is no accident the two, point and flame, coincide.

Yet Heraclitus alone among philosophers remarks on the kitchen fire, exclaiming to an astonished disciple who found him there: "Here there be gods too!" Heraclitus refers to our continual renewal from catabolism and indifference. We are awakened from dream by a need for food. Smells of cooking greet rose-petaled dawn. Strands of the lullaby are broken, giving way to daytime song. We grow aware of instinct, feeling, and thought moving within our bodies. We crave relief from a dream-filled absence. Meanwhile in the kitchen, food warms on the stove.

An open-pit fire that seared raw meat gave us our first taste of cooking. It survives in campfire, barbecue, and festive bonfire. It is precursor of the kitchen fire, warming the senses with perception in contrast to vast, cold, stellar space. It helps bring temperateness, and temperateness to us. Charring antelope or mammoth on the open plain, however, lacks an essential element of a householder's kitchen. I mean repetition. The law of the householder is repetition: The work is never done.

The law itself has a double meaning. The chores, cooking, cleaning, and laundry, collecting the trash, changing the linen, dusting the furniture, polishing the silver, can never be completed. The lack is no cause of blame but arises from a householder's inner logic. Household activity exemplifies imperfect action (as Aristotle gives it) in which one can at no time say "I am finished." It thereby holds a mirror up to a householder's nature, also incomplete.

The other meaning plays a joke. It pretends a failing, a sloth, or a passivity, afflicts the worker. A wagging finger makes light of the fact that a householder is not a hero. A hero brings things to completion—slaying monsters, invading the realm of the dead, chastising even the gods in heaven without fear. He is autonomous because he opposes himself to a flow of events. A householder is unable to entertain such feelings about obstacles. He lives with them, and they don't go away. His industry is that of a follower. A hero deprecates the position as lowly but misses the point. So far has he journeyed that home is a distant memory, not a thing of life.

To the dweller, a house is husk around a living organism and, although not partaking of life, is not itself inanimate. Its presence to a human being within both necessitates and sustains washing and wiping, feeding and drying, on its never-ending basis. Work is never done, primarily because there is no doer. A householder serves a house, and the house serves its keeper: Perfect hospitality leaves everything undone.

We of the house may enjoy rare moments of this reality when, in sponging clear a counter, we—suddenly removed from preoccupation and dream—sense ourselves the inhabitant of an unknown habitat.

In the kitchen, it is food that is primarily of fire. According to the schoolmen's law of identity, the result must already be contained in the cause. Because fire itself is like a living creature, it has appetite and needs sustenance. Cooked food is nature transformed by fire and served up for the transformation of our nature. "Ashes and garlic," T. S. Eliot writes. The animal is fed and grows docile enough to listen to essential matters. Our own substance, too, is being made more tasty for palates of higher beings. Early hunters felt the fact and took the steps necessary to prepare themselves before they stalked their game. This explains their worship of fire: Everything was for eating. The law of Agni worship is, Eat or be eaten.

Philosophers rarely attach importance to cooking. Their neglect speaks from a prejudice, early taken on. Plato notices that a mouth like ours has a dual function: Outpouring speech expresses our divine origin, and taking in food, our vulgar, lowly one. A householder knows otherwise. Preparation of food, necessitated by fire, teaches cardinal virtues of patience and wakefulness. A watched pot never boils. The stew is done when it is done and not before. But woe be to him who forgets a roast in the oven or bread in the pan—he will go away hungry. Tending the kitchen fire instructs one in the prerequisite to all knowledge: wholeheartedly following a process. To begin, find a large roasting pot, four large potatoes, a pound of lamb, a stalk of celery, two carrots, a teaspoon of thyme, a half teaspoon of basil, salt and pepper. Wash and peel potatoes, dice celery, chop carrots, cut lamb into one-inch chunks. Brown meat in three tablespoons of oil. And so on, to the savory, delectable dish that rejuvenates the spirit. Then, clean up, wash pot, put away utensils, and thus restore the kitchen to its pristine condition.

The broth, every good cook realizes, does not with necessity follow from a tempting recipe. Inadvertence, accident, and unexpectancy impart a need for vigilance. Here lies a most fertile ground for knowledge. One can trace the origin of almost all art, craft, and science to the kitchen fire. An effort to avoid contigency, error, or shortcoming fathers much deep insight. Other ages understood that a cook was to be beheaded (or to disembowel himself) for the slightest deviation from strict necessity. Knowledge, cunning, and resourcefulness thus originally vouchsafed against his death. A cook pitted his spatula against the executioner's axe. He survived by knowing how to adjust a too-salty sauce, to season an overcrisp goose, or to boil moldy cabbage. Cooking was a perilous leap from fire to frying pan, and a cook, a warrior. Along the way, the arcane disciplines of chemistry (or really alchemy), pottery, and table setting resulted.

As cook, one learns how to obey. The fire is to be tended. It is master; one serves it. The lesson leads to a distinction between need and pleasure, the necessary and the enjoyable. The lesson is universal. Food, for example, can answer to either hunger or diversion. A hungry man consumes his meal, ever cognizant of his lack, grateful for temporary surfeit. Eating in any other way means being compelled by pursuit of pleasure. By contrast is a meal partaken in need. Its taste is immemorable. I remember one long hike to the Mer de Glace on Mont Blanc when we were caught by rain. We plunged onward, wet and weary, until a small outcropping gave some shelter. There, we broke out our packet of home-cured cheese, home-baked bread, and chocolate and made a meal. No food, not even of the finest restaurants, ever tasted better or sustained more fully. With each of us, the inner person—called forth by honest physical exertion—also ate.

A householder tends the kitchen fire and is tended by it. This is taming a great power. In becoming master of it, one is forever subservient. A great animal trainer induces the mighty lion and bear to perform acts of delight by never neglecting their proper natures. He is thus bound to respect their proper feeding and care. Should he for a moment forget, his life is endangered. It is the same way with fire. One makes it a source of the agreeable and useful. It obeys. But the moment one grows in the least negligent, one sees the picture differently. In reality, it is oneself (like the animal trainer) who has grown obedient. Forgetfulness is another name for disobeying the way of fire. A burnt finger or a house fire can be payment. The nature of fire is to not forget, to show no mercy, and to restore its place to ashes.

To take the thought a step farther is to speak of our inner fire. To each thing in our dwelling place corresponds a form of intimacy. Scheler (quoting Rodin) says: "Each thing is merely the limit of the *flame* to which it owes its existence." Asked to tend our burning need to become, we apparently command obedience from our parts. In fact, in learning to feed fire, we come to listen to our separate natures, mineral, vegetable, and animal. In listening, we grow less obstreperous, less inclined to block the fire of our expression in the name of composure, reason, or desire. We then serve an immortal self and, through it, what it serves.

These are concerns of a householder. We must not forget there are many ways fire works its secret on a child. Taste in general is our sense of unknowing. A child ingests the world through her mouth. Without word or thought, the taste of a golden waffle enters her blood and nerves. The taste, once fire has licked marshmallow or potato, what worlds does it open for her? She is tamed by the experience and at the same time impassioned by it. She is, as we all are, thus brought to surrender wild appetites and, without growing cooler, to become civilized.

Eluard says: "In the bright crystal of your eyes/Show the havoc of fire, show its inspired order/And the paradise of its ashes."

11

THE WASH

Since the time of cave dwellers, we have built our houses between heaven and earth. This frank acknowledgment of our dual nature was advanced by the advent of fire, the third element, for cooking and warmth. When water, the last, came into household use is an open question. I do not include water for drinking or cooking, since it was a necessity, not a need, for animal survival. Water did not enter into human dwellings until people felt an impulse to wash. Water, mother of life—that which flows on—in the realm of a household is for washing clean.

No one writes of the wash. Occasionally, a painting from the academy will glimpse washerwomen, stuck like Brueghel's Icarus in an insignificant corner of the canvas. Even then, the wash is portrayed through romantic eyes. Billowing aprons of the women mirror laundry like water lilies on a pond. Clothes seem already clean—making the process redundant—and the river, the main attraction. But for a labor of laundering, no painter (or poet) has eyes, for this is, even in days of appliances, a most arduous philosophical work.

In a dream, nothing sticks to the skin. An infant waking from the lullaby is already clean before the light of the world strikes her. In a house (and the world around it), dust adheres to all surfaces. The bright shadow world is colorfast, but in this one, colors fade and whites turn to gray. Dirt and filth that spoiled dream life now soil clothes. In a household, laundry is necessary to confront.

Some think the wash belongs only to the character of a burgeois

69

city dweller or gentry farmer. This makes a virtue of a necessity. A starched white shirt collar may give its owner a borrowed propriety, and freshly ironed ruffles, a look of civility. In the polished facade of fascism, we may, moreover, see through the idea that cleanliness is next to godliness. An executioner may well be a fastidious man about the house. A butcher may detest stains on his wristbands. Fashion and personal sanitation strike me as the wrong place to uncover a necessity of the wash. Where else? We live in a world threatened with a more literal form of pollution than hypocrisy. Dust gathers everywhere.

Locke the philosopher distinguishes two kinds of properties a thing bears (did he almost say "wears"?). There are secondary ones like color, texture, contrast, and hue that share a trait of being lost in the wash. Whose shirt has not come back shrunken, matted, and wrung to a ghost of its former self? This state of affairs would be lamentable if the universe offered no other kind of trait. Then, either dirt or water would deny a tint and feel of things. Heroically, Locke allows other, primary properties like shape, contour, and size to be more durable. Regardless of filth or detergent powers, such attributes persist in his universe.

Such a view unfortunately reveals Locke's insouciance more than a real essence of the wash. Anyone about the house knows that garments become shapeless, undersized specimens through laundering. Their internal proportions and dimensions are no more immune to distortion than are color or texture. Shrinkage afflicts any bit of material. So does stretching, mauling, shredding, and other forms of radical realignment practiced by a launderer. Only armchair philosophy omits basic laundry-day facts from its first principles. Locke surely must have sent his laundry out.

But behind Locke's inclination lies a compulsion that rattles all launderers. Like a djinn uncorked from a bottle, the spirit of the wash suddenly looms larger than life. To it, some ascribe stupendous powers. It graciously restores articles to their proper form. It whisks away all that taints an object's true nature. It purifies by depolluting and frees by decontaminating. Householder finds himself enslaved. By what? A drive to get at the essence of things. Heat from the impulse seethes beneath the simple sight of a laundry basket, for what are stains, mud spots, body odor, and simple grime but accidents of life? Wash is a way of emptying a garment of contingency. Washed away is all but the necessary stuff. Laundry is an obsession.

What does remain? Locke is mystified by it. "A something I know not what," he confesses. A folded-up shirt, a never-used pair of socks.

Wearing an article impresses it with the humanity of our body, grease stain and all. Is this accident? Take it away, and a philosopher has every right to be stupefied. The subtraction is a way of disowning our attachment to the world. Some ideal, stainless image of how we ought to wear the cloak of mortality intercedes, blocking appreciation of a simplicity of the wash. In short, we wish not to live under the law of repetition. Nothing abides, least of all tidiness. A mess that comes from our refusal thus coats everything we touch. This is the origin of the accidental universe. We raise a dust and then complain we cannot see, Bishop Berkeley said of the affliction. He was a busy, practical man, intent on founding enclaves of civilization in the New World. Wherever men and women join together in communal life, the necessity of the wash is not to be lost.

Laundry waits with infinite patience. It has more than patience, more than action. It has being. And this because it belongs to the house. The ancient Greeks knew more of the spirit when they took the word *ousia* for "being." Eumaeus was of the *ousia*, a household or farmstead. His care for the presence of things, orchard walls or pens for the boars, was precisely and solely that which he "held." An attentive quality he brought to each thing respected its suchness, what the scholastics called its "quiddity." This inner activity is counterpart to hospitality. As a good householder, Eumaeus—putting aside dreams of his master's return—allowed things of the farmstead to come into being. Each was there, waiting with infinite patience: laundry, walkways, olive trees, even snake holes and sparrow nests. But none was as yet infused with life. None was animated save by Eumaeus's act of recognition. About this feat, it is recorded that "Odysseus was delighted to see how careful a steward he was of his absent master's property."

A householder breathes his breath into the relic of being, this bibelot, that trinket from a maternal aunt, and lo! a thing leaps into existence! Small wonder at Eumaeus's equanimity. He sensed enormous power in the part he played. Servant of being, master of becoming.

Some imagine a deep gulf between metaphysical reality and that of the senses. A city dweller (Plato is an example) is one. He places what the senses reveal on the side of illusion while the mind's eye sees truth. The world is vulgar and coarse; heaven's kingdom, sublime. The tendency speaks of a vital deprivation. Look at what an urban person suffers: An object of his sight, smell, touch, and hearing is usually artifice, humanmade elements of the environment. Horns, sirens, combustion pollutants, neon colors, plastic utensils, and recirculating air: These are human replacements of natural ingredients. We fault sensory integrity, whereas these apertures truly report a falsity of the world. Manufactured articles are only facsimiles, copies, stand-ins, pretenders. A poverty of the humanmade (which afflicted Plato too in an earlier age) can lead a thinker to an unnatural detachment. His retreat to otherworldly reality is really an attempt to palliate, dull, or subdue a painful sensory impression. You might say, asceticism is a backward way of washing the senses clean.

Has city dweller felt the texture of linen drying on the line, watched shirts billow and heard them snap in the east wind, or smelled a diffuse fragrance of cotton in a hot July sun? A body stores its own memories undefiled—unlike a mind's. The wash is always connected for me with blackberries. Laundry day in summer brings back a winey smell of blackberry, since my mother's clothesline ended in a blackberry patch. If she put out too much wash, the last sheet would inevitably come back beautifully stained. In any event, to help with the wash meant to become immersed in that magical fruity aroma. I see washing clothes as cleansing the senses, joining them to a reality adequate to them.

Lines heavy with laundry are a favorite motif of photographers. Old shots of city tenements were a paean to the wash. Ample stocks of strung-out clothes eclipse building and sky alike. Utility, maybe, but ritual enjoyment, mostly. Washers were from the Old World. Most were new to urban life. Sheets and shirts, towels and doilies, undergarments and dresses that hang between dingy brick buildings constitute memory, nostalgia, and need, all rolled into one. No launderer here doubts a sensuous appeal of necessity, or the choice of it over fantasies of heaven. Where was heaven while the wash ruled the air?

Memory and nostalgia: There is an essential connection between laundering and a remembered past. Old sepia prints and my own reminiscences both point to the same direction. Memory is a dust that collects over the garment we wear. It is unavoidable and unavoidably in need of cleansing. Memory is a great human accomplishment that has been overdone, as Nietzsche says. The pragmatists among us—city dweller, philosopher, and mendicant—fail to see how we mistake it for a living skin of experience. They forget to let the past be past.

An artist has a different, more practical idea. A wash, to him, is a dilution. Its use is in creating certain visual effects. One takes pigment (which is of the earth) and waters it down. This kind of chemistry has its magical result. What is left is not paint but its pure memory. A householder knows a memory akin to paint's memory, a memory of the other. His resolve gives testimony to it. How does he pass his morning hour? All surfaces of the habitat must be kept clean, lest an uninvited guest arrive, feel unwelcome, and depart.

I have wandered far from my mention of civic virtue. It is utility that searches for an explanation of the laundry solely in terms of propriety. Such thinking sends the wash to be done out. Inside a house, we by habit are our clothes. Trousers form and reform to the contour of leg and lower torso, a belt retains the circumference of the hips, a shirt mimics the hang of shoulders and neck. They are not extensions of ourselves, since they are penetrated by, and so thoroughly emanate, a body's resonances. They reveal who we are as much as our nakedness, perhaps more, since we are disclosed unawares by choiceless nuance.

Our being periodically submerged in a sudsy brine is a multivalent symbol. It speaks of a trial by water. How strong a taste of death can a hero stand? It repeats an action of baptism. A child awakens from a dream. Will its heart be reborn in faith and innocence? These are events on extreme poles of a life. In between lies fertility, the way a rain drives away drought and dessication. A living death of famine and thirst is the true source of suffering; the poles are ruled solely by transformation that is joyful. That which brings fecundity is purification. As the parched, dust-covered earth is washed by rains, so too the wash drives away droughty thoughts and replenishes a dry soul. The garment, however tattered and torn, breathes air again through open pores.

The purification aspect explains a deeply held habit of ours. We see almost everything in terms of exclusion and inclusion. The tendency was codified by Aristotle into logic. He thought any being either belonged to a specific group or did not. That was the law of the excluded middle. Whence does this law of sameness, so intolerant of difference as to see it solely as not-belonging, arise? We can hypothesize the wash.

Removal of unwanted dirt is an entry fee. It is an act that separates one pile of clothes from the other. It is primordial discrimination. There is no such thing as a half clean handkerchief. That is a contradiction in terms, *in adjectio*. Not only is there no middle ground on wash day. In addition, a careful launderer inadvertently sees the other stack as unwashed. Hence, a philosopher's appeal to universals, which are great piles of things, to which particulars are included or excluded. Some thinkers, however, carry a householder's preoccupation with cleanliness a dire step further. They find a source of elitism, racism, and fascism in the depolluting. A world, they say, divided into the pure and the unpure is a world in which the impure must be washed.

12

MONEY

M oney makes the world go round. In unbelievable ways, household relations revolve around money. Purchase, rental, loan, savings, investment, debt retirement, security, hope money, bribe, lease, blood money, dowry, bankruptcy, collateral. And in many names: *lucre, talents, ducats, shekels, greenbacks, crowns, quid.* Money, as I understand it, is a kind of energy, electric and gravitational, that draws us toward it as a flame does a moth. Traditional wisdom has it that love of money is the root of all evil and that it is easier for a camel to pass through the eye of a needle than for a rich man to get into heaven. When dealing with money, a householder often finds his soul at risk. What is to be done? The house is his station in the world, and money, the coin of value by which his practical affairs are measured.

A power—of Caesar's dark side—promises the commonweal for those who unleash their acquisitive instincts. War, theft, and murder are its accomplices. A home dweller keeps a house full of ghosts if he keeps his gold and silver under a mattress. Discipline is needed to keep these specters in check, a rigor of accounting. This is stewardship in the wide sense. Originally, economics had to do with management of the *oikos*, the home. A wise economist sees that money is as unavoidable as breathing and in function quite analogous. He does not hold the breath. And just as does exhalation, money opens him out to the world.

As economists, we should place money in schematic opposition to a houseguest. The pairing explains why a guest never is allowed to give money for hospitality received, and why at certain times a houseguest is forbidden to buy anything during his stay. A story goes, a man welcomed his friend on sabbath and fed him and bedded him until the new week. On leaving, the guest was presented with a bill. It read:

```
7 meals............... 11  ruples
3 bottles wine .......... 6  ruples
sheets ................. 1  ruple
soap ................. 50  kopeks
schnapps.............. 2  ruples.
```

The guest was furious and took the matter to the local rabbi. The rabbi heard both sides, looked at the bill, rubbed his beard, and said it was fair. The guest walked out downtrodden. Outside, he was amazed to see his host tear the bill to shreds. "You had the gall to charge me for my visit, which is against the law, and now you mock me. Why did you bring me here?" he said. "I wanted you to see with your own eyes what a fool our rabbi is," replied the host. "Of course you stay for free."

An opposition of money to hospitality discloses an important fact about the house. Guest arrives with news of the outside world, bargains in the marketplace, war in a distant colony, an important speculation concerning the heavens, gossip, chitchat, and coffee-klatch talk. Much can be idle or thoroughly arousing about his speech. In any event, his exchange, we saw, pries a householder from routine chores and relates him to the self. Wonder and awe again flow in his veins. He remembers whom he serves. Because of the august function, Eumaeus cautions us, a guest must be true. "Beggars in need of creature comforts find lying easy, and to tell a true tale is the last thing they wish." A task of discretion is the host's, soundness, the guest's.

Money similarly is an important arrival, always welcome. But its real movement, as anyone knows, is outward. Fleeing the meager confines of our pocketbook, it rejoins a circulation of currency, the cash flow. This is the work of money. Completing the circle, money opens a householder outward, to the others, to friends, competitors, saboteurs, entrepreneurs, lawyers, artisans, shopkeepers—to a whole history (past, present, and future) of exchange of things called "commerce." Money is literally a worldview, opening our eyes (and palms) to humanity.

It is said you can tell a person's character by the coin of his or her house. In other days, merchants of ill repute shaved and filed the edges of coins they used for purchase and sale. How one pays one's debts reveals the soul's innermost secrets. Watch avarice reach for its wallet: a cramped, reluctant gesture. Behold, the miser! Watch the fast draw of a spendthrift or gambler. Watch generosity make the same gesture, but with a good heart and compassionate understanding. The quality of one's humanity—its secret crevices and dark grottoes—stands forth in this simple act. One needs also to remember about money that it is token of soothsayers.

Disclosure of character is money's true coin. But why money when any article displays attitudes deeply suffused throughout its form and place in human life? The virtue of money lies in payment. Nothing exposes a person like having to pay. Money is the stuff of payment, and payment is the incomparable mirror of our nature. "I will give you riches if you...." Think of the villainy of Rumpelstiltskin when he had to make good his promise. Or the duplicity of the evil king when the good soldier and his six companions completed their service. Or what the burghers of Hamlin did after the Pied Piper rid the land of rats. By contrast, remember the king's delight at paying the man who made his daughter laugh. A gesture of loosening the purse strings or unfolding the billfold opens a window to a person's heart. What do we witness there? Ashes or gold?

The subject of payment brings money into focus. In light of payment, if money did not exist, we would have to invent it. Payment is an exchange diametrically opposed to that of hospitality. Look at the matter of paying your bills. You give a plumber twenty dollars for fixing the cellar pipes. But *what* is being paid for? A philosopher is the first to answer; his labor, he says. Expending mind and body's energy for the sake of an end creates value, a philosopher argues.

To modify one of Locke's examples, to hoe a plot of peas, after clearing ground and planting seed, invests the harvest with a value. The worth is different from when the peas are used for soup. The difference is apparent when they are changed for a bolt of gingham. The intrinsic value of peas is that they are for eating. This is our wealth, that the peas nourish us. A ghostly second value, potential in each pod, exists because of an act of exchange. A communist argues that exchange creates not a whit of value, any more than a picture of peas creates a dinner. Exchange of money—the marketplace—is (he says) camouflage for a parasite that feeds on labor. The disguise is a fiction and a lie promulgated by those controlling the common wealth. When they lose power, the myth dies.

One can sense a communist's secret yearning for the days of

barter. His nostalgia leads him to overlook a deeper ground of payment. We are born into this world. The meaning of our birth rarely meets the eye. In rare moments, illumined, threatened with deep loss, or at the end of hope, we recognize the fact of life. The fact is that the life we are born to is not ours to have and to hold. Not being ours, our life confronts us with a question: To whom do I belong? Like a householder, we have it as our role to care for what is given for our use, but not possession. Like the householder, we must pay the rent. The means is another of life's great secrets. To endure patiently the unfolding that is life is how one pays. The kind of *undergoing* that I have in mind has a name. It is called "suffering." By the coin of suffering do we pay for the life on loan to us.

Should one refuse to pay, suffering (as Kierkegaard noticed) does not cease but ceases to be recognized. Unconscious despair is more debilitating than conscious despair. His is, however, not a doctrine of despair; any more than household facts of dust and dirt make a theory of pessimism. One accepts the need to clean house on a regular basis. One makes a practice of it. "The householder's work is never done." Yet there are moments when surfaces sparkle with a light that exposes the essential table, the chairs, the old lamp, the chaise lounge (bought secondhand when already ancient), the picture frames. Likewise with life's things: One suffers the condition of repeated cleansing, scouring crusted edges, steel-wooling yellowed varish, abrading cobwebbed corners, and reglazing tubs and windows. Bearing maintenance of one's habitat is the way of a householder. No other exists, and it is broad and widely traveled.

A clarification is needed at this point. The suffering necessary to a home dweller's growing understanding is necessary suffering. The rest is unnecessary. Much pain is avoidable. In the ebb and flow of life's demands, there is catharsis, when the soma not burdened by the psyche's cares shows its essential lightness. These times register a payment made and recorded. The account stands better in balance. We must not forget the exceptional individual who is utterly transformed by the experience and "paid up" in the loan of life.

A careful ear will pick up resonances between money, suffering, and liberation. Which explains why the everyday spirit of money waxes so powerfully over earth. Many say sufferings have grown more numerous and intense, though more dark. Suffering is no longer the growing pains attending an understanding of one's identity. Now it is as plentiful as the mustard seed, and money its coin. We are richer in hardship as we plunder what is only on loan to us. We still could turn the debit to an asset. For instance, take alms. Almsgiving once was a legitimate means of freeing oneself from a constrained heart, a heart that makes of suffering more than it is. To give away gold was then a sign of acknowledgment. It was an interest payment on the principal that was an almsgiver's life. Modern-day philanthropy bears no relation to the office of alms, since its gifts are for the most part blood-money. One tries to buy a composed conscience rather than earn it.

Which brings us to the question of wages. A communist who is a metropolite objects to money as a token exchanged for a person's labor. He argues that no common element exists between the two sides of the equation. Labor is a use of the life on loan, and money, a usurious perversity. Socrates, who is also a city dweller, likewise objects to money offered in exchange for philosophical work, argument and dialectic. Anyone selling philosophic talents is a sophist, a peddler of wisdom.

The convergence interests me. What a philosopher sells is corrupted by the deed. He solicits payment for what cannot be bought. He thereby must confound two "metals" that must be kept separate, need and craving. The first, an alchemist knows, is immortal and unchanging. It is that which is reality for a seeker. The second is mortal and changeful. What one possesses of it never turns out to meet expectation. Socrates' worry is that the gold of the first realm cannot be bought since it suffices unto itself. To think of money is to mistake the lead of the second realm, where all worth is borrowed. A communist may be unhappy with the philosopher's terms but locates an incommensurability of labor and wages in a similar confusion. Labor expresses one's self through a reshaping of nature. To hold up a mirror earns one a glimpse of an eternal image. Wages, by contrast, are mere costs, a numerical calculation subject to change of market conditions. In short, labor costs nothing and cannot be bought.

Discovery of unlikely bedfellows points the way to another money matter on which both agree. Socrates gives us a clue. Walking with his companion Phaedrus, he finds himself beyond the city gates. He is surrounded by idyllic beauty, a burbling stream, mossy rocks, songbirds in the alders, a pungent scent of ferns. Suddenly, his thought grows obscure, and the magnificent will by which he confronts himself is blunted. What has happened? "Come, Phaedrus," Socrates says, "we must turn back. We will lose ourselves. There is no place for philosophy outside the city walls." Jarring calls of hawkers at the agora, disputations of lawyers at court, bumping shoulders with slaves, servants, and merchants, in short, the bustle and hum of commerce—doing business, buying, selling, trading, bartering, haggling—brings a context essential to Socrates' undertaking. A philosopher can seek what he needs only in the midst of a cash flow through which men and women satisfy desire. The city in his sense is not an earthly reflection of a celestial *civitas* (as it was for Augustine) but a concentrated locus of money. It is a focal point. It provides a place for Socrates to seek that which, being everywhere, has no place.

An agrarian is likely to protest. Why isn't his human enclave, in the bower of nature's splendor, a fit haven for philosophy? Perhaps Socrates is simply agoraphobic. A communist, for other reasons, knows what a farmer forgets. It is not so. He knows nature sleeps. Technology is an irritant to natural processes, rousing and making them available to humankind. A city is a triumph of technology or a scar on the face of the deep—depending on one's viewpoint. Nonetheless, the rural countryside, under snow cover, cover of flowers, fog-covered, or covered by undamped sunlight, allows a mind to dream. We return to infancy, free to imagine, to drift with drifting clouds, to sway with wind, to saw with the late-season katydids. We are comforted and nurtured as wounds heal. Small wonder that Socrates feels will-less. He stifles a yawn. He suddenly belongs to the great, sleeping body of the natural world. He has forsaken his human striving and its everyday spirits. He has betrayed his search, himself.

What of guides that, plying back and forth between heaven and earth, "weld both sides together and merge them into one great whole" (*Symposium* 203a)? Before they can perform their difficult navigation, there must be a space for flight. Ordinarily, we are little helped by the everyday spirits. They cannot serve their purpose—to relate our immutable and mutable aspects—because of an oversight on our part. We do not distinguish earth from heaven. We presume everything to be on the same level. In short, we sleep. When we look up or down so as to notice a difference, we wake. Waking, we work a transformation of nature, our own. We grow concentrated.

A new interest (and ability) to relate is the ember of a growing consciousness. Mutuality and community are newly forged implements. People have a novel need to communicate their understanding ever more extensively. How many can coexist under one roof? City is simply the phenomenal outgrowth of hamlet, settlement, and village of households. It is a further expression of a human need for wakefulness. Return to the countryside on an early winter's evening, and you will meet the peace of dreams. A city at the same hour is just gearing up for the third shift, heated argument, violence, and love. Its greater complexity has spawned many branches of technology. The one of present concern is that of exchange, of weaving a thread that keeps people together. That great invention, to render unto Caesar what is due Caesar, is money. Money is what goes round. Going round, it binds us all together.

As the communist observes, a city houses suffering humanity. Suffering is a home dweller of the city, whereas in the countryside it is merely a guest. It departs next morning with the beauty of the sunrise. In the city, it remains a bit of grey, inert debris in a bedroom corner. But the city is also an achievement—of ones who suffered to erect it. In the realm of sufferers, money is coin. Socrates, a homeless man, is at home only in the city. He must refuse to take money in exchange for his insights into human suffering. His lot is to refuse and to chastise those who refuse to refuse. Should he affix a price to his ignorance, his unknowingness, he would bring a circulation to a stop. That circulation—of a kind of irritant to human sleep and unconscious despair—passes through the many, many households and brings them to uncomfortable union. It unites clans, neighborhoods, tribes, enclaves, and blocks that otherwise might thrive on barter. It flows through their everyday thoughts, desires, and affairs, disturbing, creating woe and remorse.

The cash flow of suffering profoundly interests Socrates the vagrant. He follows it, tracking its stops, as if his course were to be always parallel in pursuit of it—but always at some remove, never touching or being touched by it. Money, the pollutant, is shunned by gypsy philosophy the way one shuns a high-tension wire. Contact kills. Socrates can no more participate in the money circulation than he can deny his ignorance of suffering. The two are inextricably connected, tied into a rabbit knot by his need to preserve each, which is the need to avow poverty. Money is the shadow of Socratic knowledge, a poor man's knowledge. It is a poor substitute for ways of knowing. Nonetheless, as the householder attests, money's poverty may still uncover the real wealth of a home—the empty brass bowl dazzling full of morning sunlight.

13

CRAFT

How to make ends meet? The cupboards are almost bare, a late frost has stunted the crops, unwelcome houseguests are depleting the livestock, the master's whereabouts is unknown, and the roof leaks. By what authority does one bring the situation under control? Not by the absent head's name, nor by force or meekness, nor even by prayer—to bring on night to thought.

A look at the pedigree of love is more promising. Resourcefulness, who fathered erotic desire, himself was fathered by Craft. Craft is a great spirit, a spirit of many talents. As slyness, he brings the three-headed hound—and the creditors at the door—to bay. As cunning, he feeds ghosts their fill of blood to learn their secrets; before, he has tied his men to bellies of sheep to escape the cannibal Cyclops. As skill, he speaks well before those having power to aid his mission. Craft is a fluid response that finds the way through the thorns of adversity. Odysseus's intelligence must have sprung from the soil of Ithaca, since his beloved steward Eumaeus possesses it in like proportion. He sends runts to be slaughtered for the guests' feast and blackens fruit in the orchards. He is ignorant—or so he says—of where vintage wines are kept and adds grains of flint to bread flour. He will obey what the times command without deviating from the truth himself. That much belongs to craft. The rest is to destiny.

Craft is the great guide of a householder. It reigns even in his absence, as it did for Odysseus the twenty years he quested to return home. Craft refuses morbid defeat. It is that which finds a way when

83

no way exists. There is only a perilous route between the Clashing Rocks and a record of all those who tried and perished trying. On the one side is a sheer cliff that draws ships violently against its granite. On the other is a maelstrom that sucks them to their watery death. How to proceed? Craft finds a way. How to pay the bills when all money is spent? How to fix a leaky faucet on Sunday? How to prepare a meal for guests when the cupboard is bare? No book of numbers, formulas, or spells has been written. Craft alone finds a way.

A strong patriarch, craft has fathered many offspring. All devolve from the master craft of running a house. A householder is a weaver, spinning loose strands of domestic life into a single fabric. A householder is a cooper, holding together warped staves when the barrel threatens bursting. A householder is a smithy, forging new tools to meet ticklish situations out of the scraps of attic and garage. A householder is a tailor, stitching together a stylish suit of clothes to meet the occasion. And so on, down the line. The many specific crafts now lead independent existences, supporting a monumental task of survival in our human dwelling place. Originally and to this day, they serve the single aim of stewardship, to maintain the keep that is home.

A household's story line does not, however, always coincide with a hero's. Like Parsifal's battle axe, craft is a weapon with two edges. In hands other than a hero's, it becomes wile. Think of Monsieur Renard of the fairy tales. The guileful fox capitalizes on another's stupidity and bags a feast for his hungry brood. The fox does not drop an acorn on the numbskull of a chicken, but seizes an ensuing opportunity to make ends meet. Aesop's fox plots a diplomatic revenge on a stork by serving broth in a shallow bowl. The fox does not design the stork's beak, but takes advantage of the design for his own end. Or the other fox, who cannot reach the luscious grapes, reaches a reasonable conclusion they must be sour. Which blade of the axe is a householder to use? Craft as a means justifies any end whatever. Only craft exercised to fill a household with purpose—of a master's return, of a guest's arrival—is higher than that of narrow self-interest. The first lends wisdom, the second bristles with chicanery.

Then there is a trickster. Knave, fool, joker, idiot, rascal, imp, all progeny of Hermes, master of masks. A trickster serves no purpose at all, not self or Self. Like time, he is a master of timing. Like time, also, a trickster is the ultimate and unique subject. His is a craft of deception, his joy is in deceiving others at their expense. His play breeds confusion, it addles the brain and creates illusion. No mean craft is this (though sometimes it is spiteful and mischievous), but at its best it is akin to the weaving or spinning of dreams. Hypnosis, suggestion, and subliminal control are powers at his disposal. Accident, reversal, upset, the unexpected outcome, the odds against all odds: All forces that willy-nilly break our expectation are consequences. They are never at the disposal of one keeping order in the home. When, after the best precautions, the soup burns or the electricity goes out just before a guest's arrival, the trickster has been at work. When the crucial ingredient has been mislaid and the new pump is a dud, that too is his craft. Which illustrates the velocity of deception, relative to our sluggish attention. We discover his ruse only through our reaction. We learn of his presence only through our absence. We are his straight man, butt of his jokes. Thus he disheartens, frustrates, annoys, and...delights.

Certain schools make a trickster's the master craft. It is a way of pointing out our idiocy. Heraclitus's image of a child playing counters—impulsive, arbitrary, random movement—fits the description. The "tale told by an idiot, signifying nothing" makes light of attempts to decipher the world's prose. Taken too seriously, such thought leads to a profound despair. Better to listen to a story. Just for fun one day, Hermes stole Apollo's prized herd. Back in his cave, he roasted a pair of fat heifers for his supper. Apollo's rage threw the heavens into an uproar. What could be the motive for theft? When he discovered Hermes, his anger was directed at the caprice, the meaningless act, the unreasonable deed, the absurdity of it all. In the name of justice, the story goes, Apollo took Hermes' invention, a tortoiseshell lyre, and regained his calm through music. Hermes became the first to buy his freedom for a song.

The fable is itself a trick. It makes us wonder at the idea of compensation, a response meant to balance a needful situation. In a trickster's craft, justice becomes a sleight-of-hand, a game of three-card monte. Hermes' real mischief leads us, like Apollo, to believe one thing can equal another—compensatory payment equals loss by theft. Thus measure—making unequals equal—first arises through hermetic playfulness. We, being as literal-minded as Apollo, accept the crazy wisdom that difference is able to replace sameness. When do we see the trick?

These two diverse expressions of craft, a knave's and a householder's—trickery and technique—are in reality not so distant. A householder's legacy was originally bequeathed to him by deceit. At the center of a house, the dwelling of *techne*, stands the hearth, which by a trickster's ploy Prometheus won from the immortals. Prometheus once had to arbitrate a dispute as to which portion of a sacrificial bull was the gods' and which, man's. He made two piles. On the first, over the best cuts, he laid the stomach, the least desirable part. Over the second, bones and offal, he put a rich layer of fat. Zeus chose, was deceived, and withheld fire from humankind. "Their home will remain cold," he exclaimed. Prometheus then worked a theft of some embers (for which he earned eternal punishment), forever warming the dwelling place of humankind. Thus were specialized crafts born from an act of duplicity.

In the home, technique, or its elder cousin knack, is know-how, or skillful means. There are those who distinguish doing a deed from the forethought behind it. An ancient division between skill and idea, practice and theory, action and contemplation, denotes a reflective attitude. A problem with the household—what to feed the guests, how to get the fire started—presents itself. One pauses before springing into action, in order to gather thought. To listen attentively for what is needed requires a responsiveness no less ample than that of an unpremeditated, spontaneous act. Thinking is as fraught with perils as doing, and the thinker is called to craft mindful thoughts and judgments, just as the hero crafts memorable undertakings. Poise, the charm of resourcefulness—craft's child—is an intellectual as well as a moral virtue.

The craft of reason enlarges the technology of a home. Thinking up new inventions, it has created the city, home of many homes. Aqueducts, sewers, marketplaces, libraries, even circuses and amphitheaters are adaptations of familiar nooks in a house. Both city and home have etymological roots in the idea of a place to be recumbent, to sleep. Both supply a refuge, a safe haven, for a person to remain throughout an interval during which ordinary wakefulness is absent. Since one is particularly vulnerable during repose, a secure keep is essential to survival. Home and city act as stewards to our everyday existence while we wander as hero through dreams, Hermes' creations. In a sense, city and home are successors to Eumaeus, crafted by reason. They ensure a return to the Mother, the matrix of ourselves, which is, reason knows, nightly renewal, replenishment, and restoration.

That is, when reason does not turn tyrant and devour its children and children's children. When it forgets love's patrimony—itself—the craft of mind may rip curtain rods from their hooks, beating them into spears, and turn ironing board into shield. This is a return to a state of nature, which is a state of war, as Hobbes reminds us. Before the civilizing influence of the house came the intoxication of chase, kill, rape, and torture. I do not speak of the hunt that was always at the service of the house. Animal death was attended by respect and love, preceded by ritual sacrifice, and followed by blessing. War by contrast is atavism, mutation of the hunt, morbidity of reason. Greed, self-aggrandizement, arrogance, and confusion are accelerants to war fire. War is demise of craft, since craft is born to serve life and desire. The cunning of great warriors is always directed toward putting an end to war. Eumaeus's master exemplifies the trait with the Trojan horse. With that strategem, Odysseus is able to begin a journey home again.

Warfare is the grotesque craft. Like all craft, it is of the home, but the home turned decadent and cancerous. War is of the grotto, the original cave, in which benighted men perceive a shadow play of dreams as reality. War keeps no philosophers, so no one can free people through a vision of goodness. The grotto changes things to the ugly and distorts all experience with pain. It is a living nightmare. In darkness, a mind is tormented by clever means to destroy itself and other minds. Rack, collar, iron maiden, water bed: all methods of slowly and pitiably putting out life bespeak their domestic origin. Hear their names. A mind's craftiness is to portray war as the inevitable human condition, a nightmare without cease. To think of alternatives to war belies a soft heart and weak stomach. Only cowards stay at home.

Yet war as a condition is fraught with ambiguity. An objector who stays on a farm with the cows knows war as fully as the dog soldier does, but a different kind. As a degenerate, misplaced hunt, war is fought in trenches, pillboxes, citadels, and beachheads. It proceeds bullet by bullet, from the air, by sea, and underground. Its issue is the corpse, the patch of scorched earth, and a mind demented from shell shock. That is the war a householder abstains from, if not dragged from his bed late one night. The other war is more silent. It leaves the dead to bury the dead and summons the courageous to awaken and die.

The inner war, the clash of opposites, as Heraclitus said, of yes against no, is kindled by a wish to end violence. The continual violation of Self is its flame. To embrace desire and nondesire alike is its cause. To bear witness equally through triumph and defeat is its weapon.

A supreme test of a householder's cunning is holy war. Neither oath nor prayer nor sacrifice of heart ever suffices to keep the long night's vigil. Knots in the hair or notches on the nail cannot tally battles won or lost. A body's fatigue or weakness is immeasurable. Yet there is one yardstick of the developing craft of warfare, a distaste for peace. The morning cleaning done without a hitch, the garden spaded without mishap, the dinner made without the unexpected: Cleverness suspects a missing element.

The truth of fatalism is not its embrace of bad endings but its respect for friction. One thing rubs against another. A grating, abrading motion disturbs the dream of life, which is endless. Being at home, one is inclined to lie down, as the meaning of home suggests. Only a gnawing discomfort of unwanted heat arouses intelligence. Only suffering for the sake of wakefulness serves this war. The rest maims the body and embitters the ego. The ultimate craft, the craft of crafts, is to mind the absentminded routine done in the empty house with nothing at risk. This is the craft of urgency, whose eye is ever on the shadow of death and who ever stalks the moment for its quiet summons to life. This is a householder's ultimate craft, the everyday spirit of his solitary round.

We are taken full circle, for what is most urgent is love, craft's grandchild. In the daydream and the brutish war ensuing, love is most urgently forgotten. A suffering of indifference is indifferent to unloving feeling. It is the lowest suffering, inert, mechanical, and self-serving. One waits for relief with half a mind. Or begs a dark corner of one's bedroom for the miracle. Too sluggish to open the door to a houseguest, one ceases to be sought. The domicile, like Sleeping Beauty's, grows thick with bramble, lost in its private nightmare, awaiting grace from a royal kiss. Prince Charming alone can redeem the capitulation.

But this way of putting it contains a confusion. The life we forget to love is our own. The craft most urgently needed is to attend life's unfolding with the same care as one has for the borrowed lamp on the living room table. It is priceless and must be returned in a while. It is a beauty (born the same day as love was conceived) that stops the eye, even as nicks of time appear—a devil wind spilling it, overzealous polishing, a child's ball. That craft finds a way to love what comes, with joy or sorrow. Never forced or contrived, it remains in a fluid state. Never consumed, it is deprived of nothing, but rather increased, by its object. It remains forever in the background, a penumbral glow to the dawn and dusk of experience.

This craft, of love, of urgency, is that of real desire. Desire lives in the absence of its fulfillment and grows fuller. Since what it seeks can never be won, desire moves restlessly about, "a mighty hunter, and a master of device and artifice" (*Symposium* 203d). Most energetic in a

still moment of existence, its ceaseless pursuit of that which lives
beyond—Life—nourishes the world. Its transit of the space of its longing opens a heart to what there is. A faintest glimpse of its object
intensifies yearning, loosening bonds of petty thoughts and vain
appetites. What is this craft, and how does a householder practice it?
He carefully wipes dust from the window each morning to let the sun
in. Shining through, the sun illuminates the care with which the home
is kept.

14

NEW YEAR'S EVE/THE FEAST

R outine rules a dwelling place. The same is true of a body. Blood without its periodic purge, the metabolism its nightly sleep, or muscle its daily exercise causes entropy to triumph. But tyrannical routine leads to a rigid posture—a body too fixed to bear a new metaphor. Frame must be ready to bend, and to bend when ready. If bedtime habit overrules the call of fiesta, slavery is victor.

The feast comes quickly and is gone, a night-blooming cereus. Its perfume may last weeks. A prudent household respects the resilience of routine; sleep is never long lost. Besides, celebration is the spirit of quickening. The heartbeat, muffled background of all endeavor, becomes a pounding drum as dance and song carry a body aloft. Ears are deafened, arteries clogged, throat choked as pulse joins thought in joy or sorrow. In a throng of feast day, one meets one's other selves. At the hour of midnight, midnight of the year, masks come off. All shall stand revealed. So, revel! Ole!

Mind is another guardian of routine. Hume was ever vigilant against mental indolence. He saw that where a fabric is rent by circumstance, mind stitches it back seamless. A gap in which yearning, hope, or care may be felt is instantaneously erased through cause of concept. The observation confirms our suspicions. A householder's daily round is fractured every moment, but his eye is rarely arrested by the fissure. Perhaps an irreplaceable piece—a borrowed lamp—catches the eye with a scratch if threat of loss is very great. Usually, nothing is new under the sun. Setting a future in uniformity with a past is the work of

91

"gentle custom." Hume saw an immense lack of reason but gave in to his addiction to causal thinking. He found backgammon sufficed to relieve the discomfort of his split vision. For he both saw truth and saw that truly he was not able to live it. Which illustrates the kinship of a philosopher to a child: Both find a game a good way to palliate the sting of reality.

To be stopped by a gap long enough to bear one's untruth: Such work makes the feast necessary. Feast is not riot, which arises haphazardly from extraneous influx, but the jubilee necessary to crown a lent of discovery. A rigid past does not clothe the present will in irons unless indifference reigns. A mental habit of shackling actions in causal chains is broken with as little as a curt glance. The moment breathes a little freer. A grave spirit has jumped off one's back. A glimpse—of possibility and power—throws light on the spontaneous birth of the event. By parthenogenesis arises each and every occasion. It has no forebears, except the whole previous history of the universe. It is born, it flourishes, it perishes. It is not caused by, nor does it cause, another event. The confusing whirligig provokes a primitive fear. Should a mind lose its grip on categories, would not anything be allowed? Anything? Aloysha, in Dostoyevski's *Karamazov*, had such a premonition. He did not see that fiesta is one alternative to the asylum. Why? Because a glance needs to enter on its own time, and life's sweets and spices fortify a body for the coming light.

Spontaneity bursts in the midst of serious contemplation. Fiesta has arrived, and he, intoxicated, is in love with the philosopher! He is all eulogy and sweet tongue and will not cool his heels another second. What else to do with him but let him talk? With wine he speaks, but no less does the philosopher. Only his is passionate intoxication, desire desiring, love smitten with itself. Whereas the philosopher opens outward—like sileni, where "when you open them down the middle there are little figures of the gods inside" (*Symposium* 215b), the new impulse opens in. It is awareness contained in itself as fulfillment to promise. Impulsive freedom enters with Alcibiades, an incarnation of Socratic musings.

A house's calendar is graduated in tortoise-slow steps. Through the houses of the zodiac, the sun makes a celestial timepiece whose light slanting on the kitchen floor makes a domestic one. Is all change cyclically slow? Routine, great ruler of households, is a performance artist who creates an illusion of uniformity. Lulled in a cradle of illusion, we are absorbed in a dream that tomorrow we will finish the paint job, continue the ironing, and begin the woodpile. Novelty arouses us. It is an alarm clock wrenching us out of night's belly and into the stinging predawn cold. Response to the shock—terror, dismay, or willingness—expresses character. Shock itself, its raw energy, is the advent, midnight herald, trumpet of the coming age. Real change, if it comes at all, comes as a leap. It is revolution, birth cry, breaking of the marriage goblet, festival, death stroke. It is difference. It is not more of the same.

Is there preparation for the unexpected? A householder keeps dancing shoes polished and suit pressed. Fantasy and vague wish are, however, not agents of urgency, real desire. The beloved advent of a hidden perspective, a concealed frame, or a veiled passageway is a vigil consummated. A mind absorbed by the round never meets a mind ever mindful of the door until "a knocking followed by the notes of a flute and the sound of festive brawling in the street" (*Symposium* 212c). In the fracas, astonishment answers the stroke of midnight. That in itself is an act of renewal, the new year's spirit. Routine confronted by its own masks drops away—like toys from a burst piñata or gods from the silenus—and confronts faceless wonder. Horns blare, drums roll, and jagged ends of a cycle, having met, themselves go on endlessly. The world stops for only a breath, but that breath is its saving grace. Then on it goes, business as usual.

Love and discord meet, Empedocles says. They encounter each other for only the briefest moment, but long enough for discord to make a eulogy. The moment is the year's midnight, and the eulogy, the world regenerated. The act is explicable. Socrates gives proof that discord is beloved of love. He modestly returns Alcibiades' affection. Concord is routine, the gray king deposed by immodesty, love's brilliant advance. In concord, friction between assent and dissent, acceptance and denial, lessens. A lullaby is sung in the key of comfort. Dream replaces a keen perception of need. Concord is a good householder's betrayer in how it dulls renewal's hunger. Only to the hungry does the spirit of the new year come. The revel that celebrates a return of light also marks a waning of the dark.

Midnight is the nadir, a trapdoor into which the sun drops. Spring it, and a plaything pops out. Jack jumps up in his box. Play surprises household work—tending door, fire, and wash—with a war whoop. Tools scatter where they fall. Discord has vanquished well-kept rigor simply for fun. A rhythm from out of nowhere moves limbs in strange, familiar ways. Tatam, tatatatam, tatam, tatatatum. Wine magically appears, a liquefaction of song. But beware! A seeker who risks oblivion in drinking also risks finding himself drunk with truth.

The temptation is to say that play is foil to work. A mystery thereby dissolves. What is a child, playing hide-and-seek, up to? If abandon reigns, poise is its consort. In distraction, play disappears into an ambient fluid, indistinguishable from random motion. The child is cut off from an intelligent play. If play is lighthearted, it is not necessarily frivolous. A boy at war play knows it to be hardly less serious than soldiering. Focus, design, and execution abound as much in play as in work routine. In fact, the self is absorbed more readily in play than in work. Play is waking cousin of the dream, motor-dreaming. Which explains that we recognize a child's play by the metaphor moving his body.

In play at midnight a child is born. In adult flesh, he dances behind an owl mask, stepping high to music, shedding lines of care etched by householding. Demand, however, is not absent from the feast, but an invited guest. If uninvited, she can, as Sleeping Beauty found, cast an evil spell over everything, a spell that cannot be negated but can only be modified. A child understands the demand that we find a contradiction, the demand to play. One is asked to don a mask, to play a role, to be owl, harlequin, princess, thief. Fiesta does not invent the peculiar aspect that exists also in a household. Instead, it puts it to good use. Working, one becomes entangled in achievement. The thought of finishing the job, checking it off the list, and taking on the next is an antidote to the free movement of child's play called "motor dreaming." Fixer, cook, bottle washer, woodcutter, bookkeeper, quartermaster: Householder thinks each role is real. His body is all business, taut and fixed on getting the job done. Fiesta demands that eyes turn up, look at the piñata. It's about to burst! One's role—householder, wage earner, steward—dangles by a string. Bindings woven of tension are unraveling. The twelfth stroke has not yet sounded. What undreamed formlessness will pop out? Who is it, really?

In the dance's midst also lurks a forgetfulness. One forgets the feast is not for free. It must be paid for in advance. This is law. It has nothing to do with a work ethic. The wedding guest of the parable, cast beyond the pale, discovers the pain of gate crashing. Walking the year of a household, one wears out one's boots before taking up dance. Deeply absorbed in scrubbing the hearth, Cinderella is awakened by royal messengers. Long suffering the misfortunes of the house, she is ready to endure more. But before, tonight must be different. Tonight must rejuvenate her flagging mind. The prince's ball is tonight.

What kind of party will it be? Grape or grain will say. Drink, being of the gods and truth, speaks eloquently. As it conditions festivity, its pleasure expresses a special voice of libation, the toast. The potent herb of language is cut into the wine, to add diction to an unspoken celebration of life. In moderation, a cup of the mix sweetens the coming spirit of newness just as it eases a labor of childbirth. Novelty also terrifies. Panic steals voice. Other than a grunt, there is no toast to mindless intoxication. (Alcibiades avoids the query, "Are we to pour the wine down our throats like a lot of thirsty savages?" [*Symposium* 214b].) A bacchanal with its orgiastic rite strives to merge all— householder, philosopher, poet, city dweller, farmer—with the One by obliterating difference. Often enough the attempt is spoiled by a contradiction. A higher unity is sought through the lower, a return to our animal nature. A besotted body is partner to no one, only the dream.

When intelligence is not numbed, toasts serve many functions: memory ("I commemorate this vessel"), gratitude ("We humbly offer thanksgiving"), appeasement ("May our conquerers have mercy"), hope ("That righteousness will triumph"), or dedication ("We commit ourselves to this campaign"). Articulate speech then eulogizes the feast. As alcohol loosens a tongue, we hear what speaks through us but whose speech is forever blurred by me and mine. We are summoned to partake and to be partaken of. A toast heralds the coming good. May we be tasty morsels of a vision that consumes all small pretenders.

With speech so direct, a toast (like an oath, a vow, or a prayer) invites great danger. The least falsity (or falsetto), and the air may be thick with thunderbolts. "I drink to the beauty of thine eyes." What if love is untrue, a mere wish for possession? Many a brilliant toast was made at the suitors' banquet, but in the end all toastmasters perished from their lies. Eumaeus reluctantly contributed his best boars. Breads and dainties heaped the tables. Wine overflowed goblets. Voice soon lost its elevation as satyrs' tongues lolled round men's parched lips. Some serving women complied. Each toast was destined to become an epitaph. As one speaks with glass aloft, so shall he die.

The feast is a dramatic play, full of fate. No accident is allowed to unravel the tale. A householder, unwitting worker of many roles, dances onto stage and knows himself as player. As Pierrot he knows laughter; as Cassandra, prophecy; as Cyrano, gallantry; as Quixote, valor. The smallest of gestures is pregnant with the part, a despising curl of the lip, a vacant look, an insincere cough. Thus is fulfilled the meaning of the feast—an event foreknown whose unfolding is not yet known. For this reason, the steward, Eumaeus, has taken precautions: All weapons are secreted under lock and key. Each guest is a householder, a suitor, a victim of falsehood. To each is about to be revealed his truth. For midnight's stroke that calls the light from darkness, we await only the voice of Odysseus's great bow. It strikes when one is least prepared.

I have nearly forgotten. The new year's eve table buckles under its load of canapes and champagne, noise makers and paper hats, party cake and glow of fire. In the background are strains of "Auld Lang Syne." Old acquaintance renewed in that fiesta is relation. Fiesta exclaims relation. Embrace, kiss, heartfelt handshake, face to face—love makes the rounds. Each person seeks the midnight moment when strife is held in balance and the play's the thing to win the conscience of a king. That organ is not a cagey censor that judges, but the faint voice of a heart that yearns. In the midst of a great battle, Socrates stood stock still through the night, listening. What he heard, he obeyed. What he learned, he became. The feast descends over one like a bell jar, and in one moment—"in the course of the same campaign"—silence roars like Odysseus's bow. A terrible fear grips all created nature. Whoever wears a mask falls like a dog where struck.

"Auld Lang Syne" plays endlessly on, an inner melody to householding. While all else changes, it does not. It is immortal. To a fractured mind, it evokes nostalgia, a sediment of feeling. Time's revenge imprisons a person in memory past. Old days glow with a displaced and false reverence. How different is a glow of present memory, the forgotten faculty. See how its background luminescence awakens joy and sorrow alike. The past is silent in the great glowing silence of the midnight sun. Rousseau's *Carnival Night* captures the moment. A line of stark, unmoving trees defines a horizon. Two figures emerge from it. Clown and princess walk arm in arm, backlit by the noumenal realm. They have drunk deeply and have let loving hands renew their acquaintance with aging bodies. They have danced, sung, and become known. Vivified, they reenter the ordinary stream with its demands of dwelling. They will linger over a fresh pot of coffee by the kitchen stove. Few words will be uttered as they hang costumes in the closet for another year. Again in their household duds, one will make a fire while the other sweeps the steps.

PART THREE

SIDDHARTHA

15

THE HUNTER

In winter dusk the Hunter rises and throws a leg over the rail fence. It is pitch dark as he glides silently over an east meadow in pursuit of the Hydra. One arm, an infinite starfield, holds a giant club. At his belt hangs a bejeweled sword that gleams of immortality. His heart is a relic of days as a human. Once he was the handsomest man alive. Now he is memory and symbol. His step is still audible, a silence deeper than the woods'. Beneath his breath, a mantra, a prayer. Its repetition is endless: good death, good death, good death.

The hunter abides in neither home nor infancy. He sleeps in the forest and, though born of a womb, he, like Athena the Huntress leaps instantaneously to the chase. Latency does not detain him. Decisive action has no phase prior to actuality. He does not pass from lullaby to houseguest to hunting. His first inbreath draws a bow backward and takes aim. Movement under his reign is ruled by a new breed of spirit, restless obedience. All spirited motion seeks union. Spirits who ply the space between heaven and earth, Plato sees, "weld both sides together and merge them into one great whole" (*Symposium* 203a). Movement is no mimicry of love but love itself. Love always takes hold of a body, divine, astral, or planetary. The body beloved of the hunter is not an angelic body or a homebody but a wounded and dying body of prey. From suffering to suffering, the hunter seeks the cause of suffering— *this* body—that he may root out its mortality. The hunter hunts death.

While on earth, Orion lived for two passions—to love and to hunt—that are one. Inviolate Dawn it was (the tale goes) whom he loved. On account of his love for her, he met his doom and found an immortal shrine among the stars. His other passion was no less magnificent: to rid the woods of ferocious beasts and monsters. In the forest lurked the objects of our fear. Behind each tree, in a shadow that forever escaped vision, dwelt the object of fear, an unknown potency. Men and women did not venture there. Human will, stung by the object, ceased to determine right thought and action. Aspiration weakened, life was stunted. Orion the Hunter was a hero called to the fear. His achievement was to retrace the way to freedom—tracking fear to its lair and confronting it for all humans. Fear that is unknown always surpasses in power fear that is known.

What is the hunter's weapon? Like perfect love that casteth out all fear, by recognition does the hunt make dark into light. That is why Orion still blazes in the winter night sky. Sword and club, gun and laser beam, are harsh emblems that belie a subtler vocation. If death is curried by the hunter's vocation, it is not of death we think. The hunter is no butcher or hooded executioner. He is a collector of traces that make up the prose of the world. The writing has been secreted on behalf of a higher purpose. All signs are hidden to our untrained eyes. Patience and perseverance have transformed the hunter's. For days he will scour the earth in search of an ancient print, a broken blade, a bent leaf. Meaning is revealed in a lightning flash, which he pursues until insight dawns. The dawning, as Orion discovered, is a death—of ignorance. What dies, among other things, is the misshapen idea the predator has of the prey.

This death concerns violence. Because it affronts our ethics of nostalgia, no other matter demands so much clarity. Often, blood is spilt. Is life thereby violated? Violence puts things out of order. The hunter follows a right order of life's needs, particularly nourishment. In knowledge, his savvy is akin to a householder's hospitality. One must pay for a meal before eating. To take without paying violates nature: One takes what is not one's portion. When pragmatics alone dictate the hunter's action, scarcity is an inevitable result. Boar or buffalo remains hidden, unfulfilled. A belly knows hunger. Life is deprived of life. All creatures suffer an imbalance.

To pay, the hunter relies on magic, a magic of sympathy. One who suffers with the other's suffering creates a debt—of gratitude—from the latter. Sympathy is the basis of all medicine, to which the hunt also belongs. Peoples who had an understanding of sympathetics saw that the spirit of the hunt ruled the healer too. In practice, a medicine person—the holy one of the clan—oversaw both activities. We must not view cosuffering in too passive a fashion, or else a healing dimension remains concealed. The healer is able to pay in the currency that the patient lacks, care. The hunter, too, cares for what the brute faces only blindly and without intelligence, its death.

Sympathy reveals that a secret knowledge governing payment involves similars. The law of similars states that what brings life to a dead creature brings death to a live one. Sympathetics gives way to homeopathics. Homeopathic action is magical to anyone who lacks compassionate vision, for, without compassion, vision remains inactive, ineffectual, and voyeuristic. Homeopathics works by the law of similars, attending to a natural balance of payments in matters of life and death, sickness and health. To the hunter, sympathy places him or her in an animal's skin. The act requires utmost seriousness. An inanimate image of the animal is drawn, and, by ritual (which is a concentration of mind), life is breathed into it. The walls of the Lascaux caves attest to the work of the animating imagination. Having been brought from image to life, a life form exists under an absolute debt to the hunter. There is nothing the hunter cannot claim as his own—even the life itself.

Sympathetic magic practiced by the hunter reverses the romantic's notion of art as mirroring nature. Mimesis or imitation is too passive for the adventuring hunter. That which is to be copied automatically assumes a higher position. The hunter's obedience is absolute: He will accept no one's dictates but his own. An aim of sympathy is to bend nature to his art. A lifeless image *will* move about the earth. A fleeing buffalo *will* assume a death pose. A homeopath's amulet contains knowledge of an exchange between vital and moribund, simple and ultimate. Thus he can offer a remedy against death.

Such art is a power. It is forgetfulness. One who forgets that all taking is self-making must pay dearly. Among artists, only Orpheus possessed the skill of the hunter. Rocks and trees, the mineral and plant kingdoms, moved at his command. Yet Orpheus, lacking sympathetic insight, failed to remember payment. His song animated things without properly adoring their lifeless state. He paid no obeisance to great sleeping Nature, from whose endless death, stone and twig had been wrenched. The injustice of his art cost him a most violent end.

Sympathy—whether in the hunt or in art—is not a feeling, but an awareness of exchange. A sympathetic imagination sees hunter and hunted, not as fixed positions, but as forces engaged in an vital dance.

Throughout the dynamic, the two change places and roles many times. Taking the place of the prey, the hunter learns the miracle of hope and surrender. In an analogous interchange, the prey tastes purpose and thanksgiving. An inexplicable bond between the two allows passage to an intelligible energy that informs both of their universal position. The hunt's outcome, moreover, is never assured. Each step counts and may be a fateful reversal. A matador lives a hairbreadth from the bull's death-dealing horns. The closer the beast passes, the greater a matador's power. All humans are intoxicated by power and by the thought of greater power. Yet to wield the greater power is to blur a line between giving and taking life. Death is the only winner in this no-man's-land. Here is another law of the hunt. The one who stalks the prey is in turn stalked by more relentless hunters.

The law of the jungle is to eat or be eaten. Over time, we both feast and are feasted upon. The only choice concerns what we are food for, heaven or earth, worm or angel. In preparation, the hunter makes herself tasty for the kill.

The Green Knight, whom some view as death, in *Sir Gawain and the Green Knight*, is a practitioner of sympathetics. A most able hunter, he challenges anyone from Arthur's circle to behead him in exchange for a like opportunity on his executioner, one year thence. Only Gawain is not overcome by fear. The Green Knight proves to be a hale fellow who takes Gawain's blow and rides off decapitated. He is a picture of health. He shows neither fear nor remorse. Homeopathically, his body receives a remedy (the death-dealing blow) productive of deathlike (but not morbid) symptoms. By contrast, Gawain exhibits dis-ease. He worries about his meeting and accepts an illicit gift of a girdle of immortality. The remedial blow, wielded by the Green Knight, thus cures Gawain of his condition. Barely nicked, Gawain jumps back, recovering his will to hunt for prey worthy of his calling.

By our motives are we tried. This is the bold lesson of *Sir Gawain*. Objects of personal gain clog a channel meant for limitless exchange. We do not broker with an unknown heaven, but with hells of greed, lust, envy, and pride. One of Gawain's illustrious colleagues of the Round Table, Sir Lancelot, demonstrates how the hunt bears blighted fruit. He and all the other knights had "each in his separate way entered the dark wood" in pursuit of the Grail. Each, that is, had taken the vow of the hunter whose prey is the life-containing vessel that brings providence to humankind—a task distantly related to Orion's. Lancelot was acknowledged to be most skilled in combat and courtly ways. Yet he had been detained in his pursuit by feelings for Arthur's wife, Genevieve. One hunt—for the realization of his immortal self—was replaced by a second—for a taste of earthly joy.

But this is badly put. One object, gold or pearl or a sage's wisdom, is no better nor worse than another if the spirit of the hunt is there. Purity of the hunter's heart, not the prey's, is what counts. To pursue Genevieve as a hunter is possible, only that was not Lancelot's way. Adultery in his case means adulteration—of his heart's desire. He follows both romance and quest halfheartedly. Francis Bacon wrote that freedom is obedience. Lancelot's waywardness lies in a divided obedience. The hunting spirit is imperfectly served.

Both hunter and hunted suffer. One evening, outside an ancient chapel, Lancelot falls asleep. As he lies beneath a bush, miraculous events unfold. Though the chapel's doors remain bolted, a light appears inside the window. The sound of the choir's celestial music stirs Lancelot, though when he tries to rouse himself, his will is powerless. Through his stupor, he beholds knights of the Grail. A deep despair takes hold of him as he tries to join the procession. He cannot move. Passing by the prostrate body, one knight remarks, "There is one who has fallen and cannot accompany us." In his distraction, Lancelot weeps with no tears.

An intensity of concentration provides a key. Taking the traces to heart, devoting oneself to watching the path, letting no detail escape: The physical ordeal of hunting confers a unity without alloys. For the one who stalks in Orion's tracks, an important transit marks the initiation. One begins with the obvious, looking *for* something or someone. Generally, one hunts for the body, knowledge, or love, which separately comprise different kinds of food. A caress, the power of knowing, or a taste of blood draws out the hunter. The matter, crowned by success or ignominy, usually comes to an end. One returns, with or without a trophy, full of oneself.

Lancelot's malaise, and ours, is marked by a lack of intensity. We are preoccupied by a thing of secondary importance. Strangely, it is what brought us to hunt, what we were looking *for*. Like a miser, however, we become slave to gold. If to obey means to follow, the hunter is he or she who masters Orion's vast vision of his starry field. A master surrenders the prey and moves on. Such a one may be asked to provide for a village or a people, but she is not detained. The sole concern is with *looking*, a vigilance that momentarily attaches to this thing or that before returning to its intense openness. No tusks, heads, skins, twists of hair, or immortal girdles decorate her wall. Preparation followed by trial returns her to prepare anew.

And what weapons? Even such as forged by magic are tarnished by a heart that refuses the call. Excalibur could show no rust or scratch from mortal combat, yet when Lancelot grew distraught, it was useless. By the same token, a rudimentary club or slingshot is weapon enough when a heart's aim is true. Technology, moreover, blurs the immaculate inner condition of the hunt. Take a rifle or shotgun. Its death-dealing efficiency is symbolized by its telescopic sight, optical, infrared, or laser. The prey is viewed as dead already, save for a squeeze of the trigger. What is served in killing through distance and indifference? Only that which is on the lookout *for* the prey. One gains no mastery of an act of no cost. One's will is slave to an image of the target. A butcher knows no sympathy for the being he dispatches.

There is another weapon the one called to hunting uses. Its blade, ever sharp, cannot be dulled by mortal things, stag, tiger, or elephant. Its enemies do not suffer joys and sorrows of blood yet are nonetheless a king's enemies. They rob a kingdom of composure. The weapon has many names, but the one young Siddhartha discovered sitting by a river seems most fitting. It is the sword of Manjusri. Its edge cleaves appearance from reality, seeming from being. To have keenness of mind to match its acuity is to recall the matter of supreme importance. It is to remember the hunt, what is being hunted, and why. Manjusri's sword provides such moments of exigency. They alone spare us unneedful killing. Any killing is unneeded if unprescribed by prayer or medicine. But it is a law that one can pray or give remedy against one's sworn enemies. They are those who make one a slave to degrading habits and rob one of knowledge of one's origin. "I have met the enemy, and they are me."

The hunter moves in silence over the winterscape. He is vigilant for traces the prey has left. It is very clever. Its habits—uncaring, mindless, self-serving ways—conceal themselves with an instinct for survival. They are not easily seen. They are his own.

The hunter watches, sword in hand.

16

RIVERS/FERRIES

Just outside the village runs the river. A road easily bridges its shallow clay banks, where willow and swamp oak also find a footing. To cross by conveyance is an act of forgetfulness. Of a space between, the river from below keeps watch, mindful of comings and goings, a memory beyond fallible memory. In springtide, it reminds humans of their lapse, swamping bridge and sluicing through cornfields. Once I saw it cover the breadth of a half mile and reveal its destiny, the sea. It was a special gray, the color of storm cloud, a vast color that shrank tree and hillock to miniature. Then we worshiped it in fear and dreaded its raw power that swept artifacts of homes before its descent.

The river spirit occupies a space between its shores even while we dispiritedly cross over, preoccupied, worried by time. Is the river also a seeker? Why else its relentless movement to the ocean? It thus reminds humans of latency as well as oblivion, promise as well as refusal. Socrates:

> It will be neither words, nor knowledge, nor a something that exists in something else, such as a living creature, or the earth, or the heavens, or anything that is—but subsisting of itself and by itself in an eternal oneness, while every lovely thing partakes of it in such sort that, however much the parts may wax and wane, it will be neither more nor less, but still the same inviolable whole. (*Symposium* 211b)

Collector of creek, brook, stream, rill, spring, and rivulet, the river runs through a channel by which water remembers itself. Separated by geology and chance, the many waters join a single current in movement to and from "the same inviolable whole." Its spirit is the selfsame power of recollection that moves between blank mountain rain and articulate river mouth, opening eloquently to the sea. Droplets strive to come together, and through trickle and waterfall their striving is made actual. Water that courses from heights to depths unifies heaven with earth, origin with destiny.

The river has sound and speaks. Its voice is vocal memory. What is stirred deep within our organism could be called "remembrance." The word itself contains a memory of origin. The Latin root *memor* (mindful) is connected with the Old English *murnan* (to mourn). A fundamental law of consciousness is therein summarized. Mindfulness exists only in a recognition of a loss of being mindful. The moment of inviolable wholeness quickly passes downstream, and we are recalled to our condition by the shock of not remembering the passage. We again discover ourselves dispersed, divided, and distracted. The river has not ceased its flow, but our attendance is elsewhere. A wondrous recovery that we call "remembrance" takes place in that instant.

"The river is within us." Cells, tissue, muscle (striated and involuntary), marrow, axon, and aureole all bathe in its life. Does the organism forget the river's search? *Our* unmindfulness is undeniable. An absence within our physical habitat is conspicuous and conspicuously a chief cause of suffering. We, the host, do not live at home. Like a ragged philosopher, we have never experienced an inner satisfaction of hospitably serving a guest and so are continually beset with queries. What are we looking for? How do we get there? Is this the best way? What will it cost?

With the river and its inhabitation, it is different. It lies in a bed it makes and does not leave it. Its quest for the sea is no different from its life movement. A scouring of water under winter ice, a rumble of spring floods, a calm pressure of summer flow: Its memory sounds in different voices. Are we able to listen? If we lie distraught, calculating a future, by its banks—the shores of our own flesh and blood—we give over to deprivation. A great restive separateness leaves no quiet. Not akin to a body's life, we are akin to no thing. The river in the body, its wail, yelp, howl, groan, or caress, sounds unheeded—though in each resonates a force to reunite us with our almost blunted purpose. If we fail to hear, insouciance crosses over the bridge, preoccupied, lost in thought, deaf to murmurous waters.

Before the bridge came to be, the river stopped people. They came forth on a mission and were confronted by what gave pause to action. The river stood in the way. In a breathing space was felt one of the most deeply human of impulses—a need to cross over. Great can be the achievement in a life, but without recognition of the need, a point of reference is missed.

Until stopped, human movement accomplishes mile after mile. A trail shows variations of difficulty within the same blind urge to keep going forward at all costs. Pleasant, scenic, dreary, or perilous, a journey recklessly invites the next step, and the next. An essential memory again erodes. What is the point of it? Plodding ahead in conquest of a few more yards prevents humans from sensing a transitory aspect of their sojourn. To be between—to be in transition—requires recognition of a hither and a yon, together with an awareness that one is at neither. Consciously plying a region between, one falls in with the everyday spirits, Socrates' envoys and interpreters that inhabit a spacious realm hidden "half-way between god and man."

To stand on one mossy bank is to grow aware of yonder shore. A broad plain stretches behind, and a second one ahead, but separated by a silver worm weaving a silken thread under the sun. The path up until now had been the conquest of distance. Now the river provides an interval, an unsupporting surface punctuated by grey heron, mallard, and waterbug. It is a new element. Subject to gravity, it is also a law unto itself, or a set of laws: surface tension, viscosity, specific gravity, aerodynamic flow. In the river's presence, a call to cross over has a threefold aspect. It is a problem of how to move in a perpendicular to the water's current. It is a challenge to a heart's commitment to continue the journey. And it is an ordeal of physically enduring trials of the passage over.

The first aspect, of a mind, invents geometry by which to map the environs and acquaint thought with a numerical image. The second, of feelings, remembers the thanks that remedy defeat and bitter wormwood. The third, the bodily, restores an adaptability lost when life forms grow fixed and settled. Fording, wading, rafting, kayaking, or floating across, we come to a new shore with newly integrated energies. A geometer's mind, a prayer's heart, and a master builder's hands gather on the farther shore. No task is impossible for them. Thus great city-civilizations have grown by the side of the river. Ur, Babylon, Calcutta, Thebes, Constantinople, Rome, Paris, London.

Song and poem are creations of crossing. Listen to Robert Burns.

Flow gently, sweet Afton, among thy green braes!
Flow gently, I'll sing thee a song in thy praise.

So is a patience for a tendentious logic whose lesson speaks of the necessity of an extra trip. A riddle to this effect exists in many lands. A man was a runaway. With him he took everything he owned. This was a leopard, a goat, and a yam. When he came to the river, there was only one canoe. It was too small for him to take more than two things at once. If he left the yam with the goat or the goat with the leopard, he would lose one or the other. How can he get all his property to the other side? Not by laziness.

To solve the riddle is to become one with an effort to cross. To clothe the river spirit—who riddles humankind stopped on its shores— in everyday garb, one plies the current between two shores. One becomes a ferryman. What does a ferryman know? Vasudeva, Siddhartha's master, says, "If I could talk and teach, I would perhaps be a teacher, but as it is I am only a ferryman, and it is my task to take people across this river." A ferryman knows of the crossing. To most passengers, the river is an obstacle, and a ferry is a means of overcoming what obstructs their attainment—to do business, visit family, or make a pilgrimage. A ferry negates the miraculous stop worked by the river's presence. Vasudeva accepts it that his livelihood is a mere convenience for most. But it also can further a momentary cessation wrought by flowing waters. For exceptional passengers, a ferryman is he who harkens to the river's riddling. "They have listened to it, and the river has become holy to them, as it has to me."

What is the secret of obstructedness? The river asks that of each visitor, but few respond correctly. To know when an obstacle is no obstacle is to discover how a fallen tree does not impede flow but detours it. Having somewhere to go, a man or woman establishes preferences. Desiring to be elsewhere or to be doing something else blocks a vision of contentment. To occupy fully each place is to answer the riddle with a whole heart. With both feet planted on firm river clay, one is immunized against an itch to go as far as the eye can see. The dis-ease (the Buddha called it *dukkha*, "suffering") is apparently an inner quivering that results from an itch. Grounded on shore, one acknowledges a mind's restless tendency and is free to comprehend the river's restful movement. This is following without taking leave or going the extra crossing.

When an urge to be in some other place subsides, the difference between the near and the far shore vanishes. One is at last able to listen to river sounds. At this far point, Siddhartha

> could no longer distinguish the different voices—the merry voice from the weeping voice, the childish voice from the manly voice....And all the voices, all the goals, all the yearnings, all the sorrows, all the pleasures, all the good and evil, all of them together was the world.

A ferryman understands how to cross the river. He who listens to the river's riddle has one himself to ask. In the fairy tale, he says, "Tell me why I must always be rowing backward and forward and am never set free." It is a question of lineage. How is a line to flow from him who has no sons and never took a wife?

The riddle of the ferryman's successor cannot be solved by logic or reason, since both point to the fact that the ferryman is already free and lacks nothing in liberation. He stayed to listen and remained in understanding. The problem of his moving on is that of making room for one who has not yet heard. If he overstays his welcome, he will grow godlike and immortal, fragile like an institution, a spirit no longer. Like the river, he must move on without moving.

Zeno presents the selfsame paradox in his account of an arrow's flight. It takes one unit of time (Zeno argues) for the arrow to cross half of the distance. To cover half of the remaining half of the distance, it takes one-half of a unit of time. To cover half of half of the remaining half of the distance, it takes a quarter of a unit of time. To cover half of half of half..., and so on. Does the arrow that appears to move across space really cross it? An effect of paradox is in fact to nullify movement—of a specific sort, a mind's. Boggled by puzzlement, thought comes to a stop. The river has again worked its miracle.

Having plied the river, a ferryman must pass on to another rung. To remain is not only to get himself stuck in a phase of the life cycle. It also is to block passage of others who ascend and descend an invisible ladder. This is Jacob's ladder, on which aspirants as they laboriously mount stone steps meet angels who lightly lower themselves from above. If movement at one rung is blocked, movement of all is affected. To each stair corresponds an understanding, from lowest to highest. To become more knowing, one must occupy the next-higher step—which means passing on knowledge of one's own position. A ferryman who unwittingly covets his role upsets the subtle communication connecting one level with its neighbor. A pathway between heaven and earth grows clogged and stagnant, a river whose source has gone dry.

The ferryman's riddle reveals an identity of his apprentice and pupil. Not by blood, merit, or desire does the newcomer inherit the position. The answer runs: "When anyone comes and wants to go across, the ferryman must put the oar in his hand and the other will have to ferry." The role is thrust into one's hands at a unsuspecting time. To want it or feel owed it is insufficient to qualify for the job, since inheritance is not a matter of logic or of desire. The river connecting heaven and earth has been clogged. At the ferryman's rung, no movement has been possible for some time. One day, you are at the river's side, needing to cross. It is sultry, and dragonflies dart on the lily pads of the landing. A craft nears the shore, and unthinking you step in. Without warning, oars are in your hands as the ferryman disappears into the forest. A life-restoring breeze cools the shore while a current slowly turns you around. Now you push off, for you *are* the ferryman.

There is a ferryman who knows no riddle and hears none from the river. He is Charon, rower of souls in need of crossing the River Styx to the underworld. His work is strictly mercenary. He will take only bodies that bear a coin pressed over closed eyelids. Coinless ones are doomed to wander forever on the near shore. Since no one comes to replace him, he ceased, an eternity ago, to be open to the notion of moving on. No longer a spirit, he is a functionary. He speeds across the surface on his skiff. With a clerk's sullen wrath he greets Dante, who waits to cross to Hell's gates.

> By other windings and by other steerage
> shall you cross to that other shore. Not here! Not here!
>
> (*Inferno*, 3.90)

Even after Dante boards and the ancient hull rides more heavily "than it had ridden in all of time before," Charon makes no move. He forgets to throw the oars to the living man he transports across and to leave the boat himself. He has lost his chance. The River Styx is silent and hateful. It lacks a source, and its mouth never empties. Those dispirited ones who cross never return. They, therefore, take no memory of passage, nor is one given. The river is a river without memory. One of its tributaries is the Lethe, the River of Forgetfulness; when passing over it, we feel lethargy. Charon's ferry is a low point on the earth.

Small boys play a game on the bridge. It is high summer, and blackbirds chirrup in the willow grass. A brown stick becomes a water snake slithering below rocks. The game is timeless, and the boys give no thought to where they are. Drop two sticks into the upstream current and run to the other side to see which comes first. At times, only a single stick emerges. At other times, two come tangled as one. Sometimes the boys do not know which stick is which. A bantering stream moves back and forth, with and against the current below, a wind of sorts that never strays from midstream. It is a river song, a song of enjoyment.

Excitedly, the boys reenact a memory. The game is an ancient prayer. They place their joy at the disposal of the river. Whose offering does the river find most generous? Whose does it spirit away most quickly? Throwing his seine to the tide, a fisherman performs a similar ritual but lacks the purity. His contains an ulterior request for his catch. The boys simply drop an honored trifle and read the river's answer. "Yours." "His." "Neither." "Both equally." They watch, it tells. It watches, they tell. They pass over their sticks that pass on the river under them.

To pray is to wait, watching. The telling happens. This or that stick, or no stick at all, appears, and that is the telling. While boys dance a river dance and the river dances beneath, the praying goes on. Its basic rhythm was present in a nursery bedroom and is present still as the boys figure out the winner. Memory is always winner, triumphal return to a concentrated flow of energy passing endlessly down from source to mouth.

17

ROPE

In summer twilight, a single length of rope hangs from the maple tree. Against a copper sky, dropping from an overhanging branch, it dangles a thick knot a foot above the river's current. Fading light catches an unmistakable plait, differentiating the rope from a vine or strip of bark. A breeze plays it back and forth like a child's game, so that one can almost hear small boys shouting excitedly from shore. Bare feet gripping a knot, they swing down and out and over clear water before abandoning themselves to the freedom of a dive. Rope is for swinging.

Hanging from bough or pole, rope connects above with below, the lower with the higher. It is made to climb, shinny, draw up, mount, or ascend—or drop down, lower, or descend. Rope mediates the heights with the depths, moving easily between levels. Passing through the middle space, rope connects center and perimeter in a spirit of oneness. In this way, it joins the work of spirits, needed (as Plato says) because "the divine will not mingle directly with the human, and it is only through the mediation of the spirit world that man can have any intercourse, whether waking or sleeping, with the gods" (*Symposium* 203). Freeing our human aspect to avail itself of a movement originating in the undying realm, rope gives force to the boys' yelp as they plunge into icy waters. The moment of flight is of joyful union.

A knot too is an accomplishment of rope. A length is compacted by lacework and made to serve the purpose of holding together. What

113

once joined earth and heaven now knits together many worldly things. Knotted rope retains a power with respect to movement, the power to arrest it. Once in a knot, things stay knotted. Craft is wily and composes many, many knots, corresponding to many purposes. There is a vast family of knots: clove hitch, granny knot, figure eight, fisherman's bend, slipknot, half hitch, stevedore's knot, surgeon's knot, true lover's knot, and Turk's head, to name a few. Each knot is a conundrum. To tie it is a skill, to undo it, a challenge fraught with danger. Apply the wrong force, and the tangle is tightened. What is held by a knot may no longer be extricated. A hero who tries to untie it may find himself under sentence of death. The knot becomes an emblem of permanence.

The power to bind things together, like with unlike, is great. It is to harness a motley association of objects, one to one, and to lend direction to the assemblage. It is to humanize nature. An ox wanders the field until yoked to a plow. A pack falls off the back until strapped securely on. A bow has no backward bend with which to impart force to an arrow until it has been strung. The drift of things stayed (or their collision forestalled), human will to achieve makes new conquests. Knotted down in places where it threatens disorder, the world is made to serve farmer, engineer, architect, mariner, and soldier. To tame a wild horse, knot a rope halter around her neck. Thus rope makes a place on earth for us.

Diverse accomplishments follow from rope's teaching of making unity out of a multitude. To an infinite variety and difference of things correspond the fragments, accidents, and enigmas that compose our lives. High aspiration meets petty grievance, compassion meets miserliness, and love meets hate. Being many, we lack the oneness conferred by a roped knot. Thus a craft of joining part to part and part to whole came to be and was called *yoga*, a Sanskrit word for "to yoke." "I yoke myself, like an understanding horse," says the *Rg Veda* (5.46.1). By a tenacious keeness of mind, a *yogi* binds disparate elements together in a true lover's knot of unity. Like splayed strands of a cord, we come unraveled when vanity assumes high importance. Maker of knots, the *yogi*, empties himself of himself and lets craft take precedence. A knot maker is, therefore, master of both discipline and sacrifice, the latter to "offer up all the workings of the sense and the breaths in the fire of the *yoga* of self-control, kindled by gnosis" (*Bhagavad Gita* 4.27). Preoccupation with the foreground of self-will gives way to an awareness of a vast, omnipresent oneness.

The powerful spirit of rope binds together a life, whether by happenstance or by intelligence. We are descended down the birth canal attached to a rope grafted onto our middle. It marks the point of our entry, joining infant and mother in that moment, and infant to the earth. The mark, of the navel, remains throughout a life. It is a signature of both the central and the mortal. It is the point around which our creatureliness revolves.

At birth, roped to our center, we are prevented from flying back to the angelic realm too quickly. The dream, the play, the home dwelling, and the journey—accoutrements of mortality—must first be enjoyed and suffered. No choice is given in this gift. The cord is also a tube through which a taste for life on our planet is nurtured. Feeding has gone on for many weeks before birth. The cord is severed only after the midwife ensures the newborn of its first breath and cry. Having tasted of food of the earth's atmosphere, an infant can no longer rise to the celestial level without long preparation. Rope and its cousins, string, twine, and thread, imitate an umbilical cord. Wrapped properly around, they secure, keep, and protect from loss. If wound, say, around the neck, they strangle and bring forth stillborn what was destined for life.

As we enter roped, so do we leave. Rope attends the body, lowering it into a waiting grave. A quiet requiem of coffin meeting open ground is sung by rope paid out over the mourners' hands. Lilies, reminiscences, and eulogies are different keys to the song. The mortal coil is no longer bound in partnership with a yearning for liberation in this life and dissolves to its elemental forms, rejoining earth's crust. Sometimes, however, the sound of rope is percussive. On the gallows, justice is summoned with a roll of drums and clash of cymbals. A hangman's noose is a knot I failed to mention. It also is crafted with knowledge of human anatomy and of the physics of falling bodies. How it is knotted, the executioner knows, determines the drop and swing of its victim's death. Its precise loops are a work of macabre beauty and of universal meaning. Yet empty in twilight, swaying in a breeze, it has every bit of the look of the young boys' swing.

Against a sea of change, the power to keep in place is among the greatest possessed by everyday spirits. A rowboat moored away from the river current, a kite testing the wind's will, a tent secured by its ridgepole against gravity—rope is able to challenge such prodigious tides. Without rope, the drift of things across the worldfield would allow us no more home than smoke is given. Even a nomad would have no assurance his scant belongings would stay on a camel's back.

Secured and stabilized, things can be known, used, and loved. Thus do all knots derive from the true lover's knot.

The keeping power of rope is akin—as the word *keep* tells—to that of the look. An outward look fixes things in their places for the millisecond needed to give them form. That they then move on, change face, and transmute does not affect the keeping, since what is kept is a representation, not the thing itself. By seeing a black, sleek, slithering mass as "salamander," the look confers the same permanence on the creature as would a rope. The reptile escapes the noose of everything but that of naming. It would crawl away in underbrush and become a hidden part of a rushing, undifferentiated ground. The thread we hold when building the edifice of science and technology, for a grip on things, is (as an infant discovers) important in order to be nourished by our life. In this way, an invisible thread of the look is a replacement for an umbilical cord. A pupil is a kind of navel.

A rope is a thing with two ends. What rope keeps in place also keeps the one who holds it. I hold a dog's leash, but it also holds me, as long as I want to keep the dog on leash. The same holds true with the nominal thread born of a look. The glance that catches a salamander in the slender lasso of *salamander* is also kept by the same cord. Even after the wriggling disappears, the word remains in thought to cloud perception. We think "salamander" while confronting bland faces of lilies of the valley beside moss-covered rocks. The name echoes in a mind, rope cannot be let go of. A magic spell, once known in childhood, that can undo the knot, has been lost. Abracadabra, and the look is cleared, the names loosened from a mind. But alas, we now lack nimble, keen fingers. Thus are we kept at the same time as keepers.

To become agile again is to restore a function of active oblivion. The look identifies what there is, but without attachment. Bondage by rope supplies the challenge for a Houdini. It incites him to action. His art of quick escape acknowledges rope's binding power but knows how to unwork it. What is his *yoga*?

> The childish go after outward pleasures;
> They walk into the net of widespread death.
> But the wise, knowing immortality,
> Seek not the stable among things which are unstable here.

> (*Katha Upanisad* 4.2)

The look darts out and takes an object, but because of a supple grip, Houdini is not a prisoner. Just when we are transfixed, he is alerted to possible capture. They have put him in a straitjacket, legs and thighs roped together, eyes blindfolded, a noose around his neck. Then they throw him in the river, weighted with rocks. As he sinks, he stoops, weaves, contorts, reaches behind his back, and lo! he is free. His trick is trickery only to naive eyes. It is in reality a study of the rope spirit. What binds is what frees, and what frees, binds, so long as this study is in force. Grip a noose and be gripped by it. Let it exercise its grip on you, and a possibility of escape arises. Such leniency redounds with Houdini's hope.

In it also lies a riddle. A man keeps a slave at the end of a rope. How many things are there? Since captive and captor are interchangeable, they are not two, but one. The proof is this: Should she escape the rope, her captor is compelled to seek her recapture. Is he different as long as he defers to her captivity? They become separate things only when rope is keeping them so. Then, keeper, kept, and keeping make, not three, but a unity. Herein lies a secret of Houdini's compassion.

As retainer of things, rope bestows yet another great gift to a sojourner. Within constancy of change, the knotted rope allows one to keep track of days and moons, miles and immeasurable phenomena of the night sky. If not the invention of rope, the count was preserved by it. Tie a knot for each watering place or each sleep. By the end you know how many stops it takes from Damascus to Jerusalem. Being able to keep a tally is a door to the sacred realm of numbers.

To have a count of numbers means fewer things escape the keep. Unless you know how many sheep, a flock may be slowly devoured by wolves. If the weeks are not tallied, you may miss the propitious time for planting. A new kind of measure is given by numbers, quantity. Important devices follow. A measuring rod is just a knotted rope made rigid. A calendar is its tableau. Fields and highways, lunar eclipses and meteor showers, could now be tracked. The count gives new meaning to the sense of a lawful cosmos. What is lawful can be counted, and all that happens is countable. Thus lawfulness of phenomena is precisely what may be counted on.

The discovery of quantity led to the early sciences of Pythagoras: arithmetic, astronomy, music, and philosophy. Here, the count lies behind the workings of stars, song, and thought. An early flowering of knowledge recognizes the count as mediator between heavenly precision (perfect differentiation of strands) and earthly inexactitude (blurred boundaries, overlap, and tangled threads.) A thing's essence, its number, determines its hidden place in reality. Proper study of

number, however, enables one "to disregard the eyes and other senses
and go on to being itself in company with truth" (*Republic* 7.537d).
To seize a counting rope leads to liberation from murky appearances.

To speak only of rope's accomplishments is an easy temptation.
Being so many, they belie the simple rope itself. It is no single strand
but a braid of three or more. That rope is an interweaving is one
source of its strength and endurance. Just as an umbilical cord comes
from a mother's body, the woven rope—its copy—belongs to the fem-
inine. *Weave* and *woman* share a common root. A spider at her web
like Penelope, Odysseus's faithful wife, at her loom recalls the fatal and
cunning work of rope. By unmaking her tapestry each night, Penelope
patiently deters the suitors until her husband's return and their death.
By remaking her web each day, a spider lays a deadly trap for her prey,
her life's renewal. By their skill, both keep to a purpose in face of
adversaries' threats.

A weaver's rope holds a strategy. Therein lies its beauty, one
strand placed over another and drawn under a third, carefully over and
over again. A strategy is a way and a map—what Ariadne hands Theseus before he enters the labyrinth. She offers a ball of thread, a rope,
she has woven. The underground maze is a tangle of blind alleys, dead
ends, pitfalls, and quagmires. It is the life inside himself that he is to
penetrate. At its center lives a monster, the Minotaur, half man, half
bull, that demands sacrifices to its grotesque appetite. To succeed is to
keep track of his journey. Ariadne's thread is guide to Theseus's heroic
quest and midwife to his own birth. It is an example of rope's power to
unriddle the self.

To every rope is assigned a length. The length—to which corresponds the life of each thing—has been cut from a single unbroken
string, the proto-rope, that comprises the manifest universe. So modern physics, with its "string theory" of reality, concurs with ancient
thought. The length of a tree's time is a few score years; a moth's, a
few hours. For each being, rope stretches only so far. What happens
then, at breath's last breath, turns on an understanding gained during
the full length of breathing. Total dissolution, nothingness, or continuation in some form or formlessness—it depends on the fidelity with
which one has sought one's place and accepted an infinitude of other
places.

A puzzle surrounds the job of dividing the master rope. The
immortals cannot divvy it out, since they too have their day and are as
subject to its length as we mortals are. The ancients tell that lifelines

were prepared by the three Fates, braiders of rope. Clotho spins the flax, Atropos twists it into thread, and with her shears Lachesis snips it at the measured length. They are tireless and never sleep. Their intelligence, finer than the gods', knows the points of the rope's natural divisions. A vast netting of all things, knotted at the joints, forever guides their hands as they cut rope for each place. The net is an image, a luminous energy. It is Indira's net on which hang all things, past, present, and future. The net alone survives all transformations wrought by the Fates, since it is a template of roping, not rope itself. The Fates themselves also have a lifeline. Like all else, they cannot outlive their day and function. When all rope has been cut to length and the manifest universe ended, spinning wheel and shears dissolve, and they too return to sleep undisturbed by dreams.

Whether the Fates provide material for tragedy, theirs is (as is tragedy) nonetheless a play. "This play was played eternally before all creatures," Eckhart writes. It is pure because, being playful, it desires to secure no particular end, as does a work. Interwoven elements of freeplay—dream, fantasy, apparition, or mirage—move free from any pragmatic, creaturely design. Liberated from the frown of thought, we humans engage joy of play through *yoga*. We are able to play when "mastery is of action only, not of its fruits; so neither let the fruit of action be thy motive nor hesitate to act" (*Bhagavad Gita* 2.47). Such play then is not separate from, but marked by, seriousness of commitment.

Watch a double length of rope swing rhythmically between two young girls. The sidewalk is flooded with spring sunlight, and shoes shuffle on the pavement. Rope is for play, and its contrary movements exemplify how closely work dogs play, or labor steals an aimless joy. The girls sing as they jump.

> Seesaw, Margery Daw
> Jackie shall have a new master
> He shall work for a penny a day
> Because he can't work any faster.

The song, too, forewarns of the interplay. The game of jump rope is momentarily uplifting before enroachment by work, fixed ends, ideas of achievement, and refusal of the Fates. For the duration of rope's song, we are alive to our old master, the one before the one that gives a few pennies for work speedily completed. But it is the coppers that we think keep us going. Rarely are we turned from chiding a child for playing to turning to it with wonder and awe. "Are we to live always at play?" Plato asks in such a moment, "and if so, at what sort of games?" He answers: games "such as sacrifices, chanting, and dancing, by which we can win the favor of the gods and overcome our foes" (*Laws* 803d).

The spirit of rope, stretched from earth to heaven, may be played to our human advantage. Toy, plaything, or instrument, rope resonates with an animating force of life. Does it not even *look* lifelike, since it is sometimes mistaken for a snake? Our journey in a twilit unknown is made possible by its help.

18

SHADOWS

R arely does one walk alone. In rain, under thick cloud cover (like a god), in fog, by predawn light, with crepuscular evenfall, or under stars and a silver moon, solitude exists. Deep woods also bring mystery and fear of companionlessness. All things touch an inner surface from up too close, as if the well-lit world drew sense to it and diffused a hidden terror. Is that so?

> Self-activity pierced the openings of the senses outward;
> Therefore one looks outward, not within himself.
>
> *(Katha Upanisad* 4.1)

Or is it just a confusion of space that assaults us while hand and foot grope for touch where the eye effortlessly photographs a vista? Then things startle us in their nearness since they are imperceptible until pressed upon the skin. Unprepared, we feel invaded, penetrated by presences we do not anticipate. This state is an infancy. Knowledge by sight has been surrendered, and with it a trust in image, portrait, and visual representation. The learned trust is abruptly replaced by an unlearned one. We come back to a more primordial inheritance—a power to sense existences directly through the pores.

We are mostly protected from confrontation and question. In light is companionship, though in truth it is not light itself, but what hides from and in it. This everyday spirit gives immense solace to humankind and thus is of two values. It helps by keeping us in move-

ment, free from a paralysis born of terror. But it turns us from our contradictions, our unknown destiny. Its duality belongs to its essential
nature and is cause for an immense fascination it holds for humankind.
I speak of what beguiles every small girl and boy, in dream and in
broad daylight and into adolescence, when rituals of adult life super-
vene. I speak of shadows.

T. S. Eliot dares to recognize our shadow reality:

> And I will show you something different from either
> Your shadow at morning striding behind you
> Or your shadow at evening rising to meet you;
> I will show you fear in a handful of dust.
>
> (*The Wasteland*)

The double is a companion, compliant, mocking, agreeable, as excitable
or passive as oneself, familiar. It is reassuringly separate yet never causes
harm. If shadows are darkness, they are darkness that appears only in
light. That makes them light's darkness, not dark's. And the dark's? The
labyrinthine void holds monsters who never cast shadows. That which
light never reaches is the shadow side of shadows. Physical exhaustion,
emotional duress, torture, high altitudes, heat, or extreme cold may
leave a trapdoor to the maze open. "Who is the third who walks always
beside you?" asks Eliot. Then even shadows of light fade in an intense
interrogation of a realm beyond companionship and duality. In what
place is our place?

By and large, an otherness of shadows does not disturb our
dream-bound day. Shadows that grow from the north side of a mountain and the south side of a river complete a pastoral beauty. On the
opposite side (south with the mountain, north with the river) light elon-
gates. To a careful eye, in the shadows' heart grows a lightness that has
been given back by reflection. The dynamic balance puts ancient Chinese thinkers—those dreamers—at ease. Dark and light, *yin* and *yang*,
compose a whole in which each shadows the other. There is no disap-
pearance that does not issue in an emerging appearance. Risk is an aes-
thetic concern. The world becomes a Chinese watercolor, a brush stroke
of a balanced moment, peaceful and quiet. A dragon, shadows' other
side, the side that never touches the sunlit lake, has been banished forever. It plays no visible part in the dance of firm and yielding lines.

A lake, ringed by cypresses, stands beneath a towering mountain.
In the distance, a lone fisherman rests his oar against a landing.
Motionless, he is already in movement. In the same way, dark ink

strokes move in the still light and chase each other like ripples on the lake. Dark shadows, and is shadowed by, light. When we recall that *shadowing* is an action, the painting reveals a darkness born of sunless caves and grottoes. Figures—the fisherman, his boat, the cypresses—are pursued relentlessly by a background that refuses them peace. One thing is tailed by its opposite, tranquil by disturbed, open by closed, hopeful by despairing. Nothing is let alone, unless it is the selfsame struggle that rules the tableau.

Herein hides the monster—of Theseus's quest—that threatens to devour all things, to reduce the painting to blankness. Its nature too is dualistic. The Minotaur is half human, half bull, intelligence mixed with craving for blood. It shadows us who, accompanied by faithful shadows since childhood, live in the sunlit world. The Minotaur, the other face of shadows, is a force of unmaking. It goes by other names—*chaos, entropy,* and *destruction*—but they all mean the same thing. The Unmaker takes a thing back to its beginning, before it was formed, known, and weighed. The Unmaker undoes existence.

The secret duality lends shadows another property. Shadows are for hiding. The delight of a small child who hides in the shadows in ambush of her mother! Concealed, she can see but is invisible. Protected and empowered, she works her will in play. Light cannot find her, but she is with herself. This is mischief, but what of invisibility combined with absence? Things hid in shadows of ourselves are neither found nor known. Yet they share one aspect of a child's delight: They watch for their chance to spring themselves upon us. The vigilance of wrath or fear that waits unseen for years before raging to the surface is helped by shadows. Shadows are protectors. Such proclivities are unable long to survive the scrutiny of a shadowless intelligence. At noontime, the lengthened shade of dusk shrinks almost to the vanishing point.

But if vision is never exercised? Dante's hell is populous with passivity. As he explains,

> all who die in the shadow of God's wrath....
> Divine Justice transforms and spurs them so
> their dread turns wish: they yearn for what they fear.

> (*Inferno* III.120)

Concealment is their state of being and such beings become the shadows of themselves. In the inferno, they perfectly express their habits of hiding—fraud and violence, wrath and greed, theft and carnality—

with nothing left over. Lacking substance of change, they are substanceless, and their repetitious acts come to no resolution and leave no residue. Thus at Dante, intent on exercising discernment, Charon the ferryman scowls, "A lighter craft than mine must give you passage" (3.90). Dante, who casts a shadow in light, has physical weight and the possibility of decisive action. His is a problem novel to Charon's boat, which is burdened by a grave but weightless dread. It is Dante's flesh, his body, that is summoned by gravity and makes a difference. Others, who no longer cast shadows in light, are yet shadows—now of the unlit. In their erring, they have embraced the other side of shadows' duality. They are nothing but hiding. Each act tells of their unmaking the light.

With each loss of illumination, we move toward shadows. It follows that every dimming of a total, explosive, and all-encompassing revelation that began the beginning is a surrender to shadows. Only in beginningless time are there none. Once a cosmic clock is set in motion and an Original Impulse given over to lawful interaction, there must be eclipses, occultations, darknesses, and places to hide. Let there be light. Let there be brilliance sufficient to disclose each thing in its truth. In the primal act concealment is also created. Plato tells that light is the shadow of God. Radiating from a source, light must have a direction. Where it reveals an object, it is stopped. Thus in the created universe every disclosure involves a cone of hiddenness. Each truth momentarily uncovered provides a new hiding place. Dante's souls hoarded gold that turned to ashes in the grasp, and then hoarded the ashes' ashes. Their pain was in that.

In God's shadow, a child laughs. "On the seashore of endless worlds the children meet with shouts and dances" (Tagore). Too elastic for habit, a child weaves her play with strands of fact and dream. The shock of revelation and the comforting sleep of shadows do not evoke the reactions of adults—we who seek pleasure and avoid pain. On the seashore, wave after wave crests with truth and is shadowed by a trough of hiddenness. In these waters a child plays. She is not oblivious to the rhythm as she is buoyed up and let down. It is her dance in which eclipse of and call to light coincide. So it is with those infancies that do not dwell on hiding but pass it over for the next recognition.

A mix of truth and lie in the visible world wakens a need for discernment. Siddhartha sits by the river for hours to study the movement of shadows over the depths. Their image gives a play of reality but is not real. How to pierce the veil of illusion to the Self that waits in composure on the other side? "By images I mean, first, shadows, and then reflections in water and on surfaces of dense, smooth, and bright texture, and everything of that kind, if you apprehend," writes Plato (*Republic* 510a). An unchildlike distrust of shadows lurks in the thinker's thought. Plato's divided line says that shadow is lower than that which it shadows, and that which casts a shadow itself is a shadow of things veiled from sight. Like Plato, Siddhartha's first approach is to look behind *maya*, the shadow play. To rend the veil with razor-edged argument, austere reason, and dialectic is to battle one's way to heaven. This way is an ascetic's.

An ascetic's denial is of shadows, outer and inner. His words sound harsh to a child who knows companionship and love of shadowy things. Listen.

> And the release from bonds, I said, and the conversion from the shadows to the images that cast them and to the light and the ascent from the subterranean cavern to the world above, and there the persisting inability to look directly at animals and plants and the light of the sun, but the ability to see the phantasms created by God in water and shadows of objects that are real and not merely, as before, the shadows of images cast through a light which, compared with the sun, is as unreal as they—all this procedure of the arts and sciences that we have described indicates their power to lead the best part of the soul up to the contemplation of what is best among realities. (*Republic* 532b)

Rejection of friendship breeds a hermit's reclusive heart. A hermit combusts all infancies in the fire of austerities. His practice is to root shadows out from their home on earth and cast eyes toward shadeless heaven. What look do his eyes convey? Deprivation of a fullness that shadows him. Obsessive honing of a mind does not dull one's hunger for life, only one's embrace of hunger. Self-willed extinction of shadows has the good fortune to meet a built-in safety mechanism. When the breath is held overlong, one blacks out. Respiration begins anew as body reasserts itself. (It too is a kind of shadow.) So it was with Siddhartha. Abstaining from earthly life to the point of death, he was buoyed by what shadowed him, forgotten—his love of ordinary things. He awakened one morning hungry from self-denial and accepted a bowl of sweetened rice that nourished him.

The mystery of shadows beguiles a child's mind. What trails a man at sunrise, sleeps at noon, and walks ahead of him at sunset? What mimics him perfectly, cannot live without him, yet does not exist? But the shadow's riddle is not for an ascetic. His desire is to turn from shadow play toward the source of illumination. Listen.

> When one was freed from his fetters and compelled to stand up suddenly and turn his head around and walk and to lift up his eyes to the light, and in doing all this felt pain and, because of the dazzle and glitter of the light, was unable to discern the objects whose shadows he formerly saw, what do you suppose would be his answer if someone told him that what he had seen before was all a cheat and an illusion, but that now, being nearer to reality and turned toward more real things, he saw more truly? (*Republic* 515d)

Imagine him at a Balinese puppetry performance where the theatre is being enacted all in shadow. He squirms in his seat, trying to figure out how it was done. The contrivance is wasted on his boorishness. The show is not real enough for him.

A mysterious attendance of shadows in our lives gives a clue to one not hobbled by curt rejection. What in us is able to encompass both source and shadow? Siddhartha sits on the edge of shade, sun directly behind him. He looks at his shadow. Gradually, two things strike him. The shadow that looks perpetually into earth never returns his gaze. Since reciprocity is never complete with the shadow, the shadow is no complement but a repeat. It is other but, like an echo (the shadow of sound), without resistance or disagreement. It is not real. Its otherness too is shadow, for meeting the other face-to-face—either with or against one—confirms he is not oneself. When one moves one's hand, the other may not move his. In this mystery arises difference.

Siddhartha is not yet through with his contemplation of shadows. As he sits, he watches his shadow body from behind. This affords him a vision otherwise inaccessible to his sight (save in reflections)—of his back side. To behold the shadow is to see of oneself what never meets the eye. Parts of the shadow facing Siddhartha are of the backs of his head, his shoulders and torso, his hands. His look is always from the rear. His shadow never turns: In this fact resides a tragic element. Within his (and our) world, the shadow does not take on an impression of human life. It is continually looking away. Catharsis and purgatory may bring about a 180-degree reversal in its attitude. As of now, passivity and blindness toward its predicament mark the shadow's existence.

This fact reveals two more aspects of the shadow's riddle. To move by imagination from shadow to flesh, from Siddhartha's shadow to himself, requires passage through to a new dimension. The dimension is unknown and unexperienceable to creatures of shadowland. A casting of shadows is possible only by shrinking the number of dimensions down to that of a shadow body. Shadows suffer the loss. That which is lost is body, the space of the organism, cell, tissue, and plasma. Human shadows, confined to two dimensions, obey the laws of a flat surface. Their communication with us, therefore, is marred by an incommensurability. When they speak, as it were, they seem to remind us of something not quite graspable. Though forgetful, we who inhabit a body cannot entirely absent ourselves from our organic habitat. It is that which they recall us to.

That shadows present rear views of oneself opens up a field of reversal. What goes one way may suddenly go the other. The uncanny feeling of facing two opposing directions at the same time—forward and backward—comes with shadow watching. Perhaps the freedom explains a child's love of shadows. Ordinary boundaries blur, known positions waver in time-space. Am I the shadow or the watcher?

The question expresses a felt sense of being under surveillance from the rear. If there is one who watches us as we do our shadows, it belongs to another, higher dimension. Relative to it, our reality lacks a counterpart to the organic substance that shadows lack for us. Furthermore, like shadows, turn as we might, we cannot face the unknown interrogator except by reversing our line of sight. We need to stretch toward its height. In relaxation and abandon comes reversal of contractile habit—what keeps one pinched, flat, and shadow-gazing.

> Now the light which shines higher than this heaven, on the backs of all, on the backs of everything, in the highest worlds, than which there are no higher—verily, that is the same as this light which is here within a person. (*Chandogya Upanisad* 3.13.7)

That the world is backlit creates shadows. That its lighting is from the back makes this everyday spirit important and endearing. Its call gently awakens a child's affections, much as it terrorizes a world-weary adult's. The spirit is selfless. It wishes us to turn from itself, toward the source of all shadowings.

19

THE DESERT

The desert is upland from the river. No waters cross it in their earth-bound form. Drops boil up from the stream, evaporate, and are carried invisibly by wind to mountain passes guarding the other side. Snow, then spring rains, deluge the valley as river waters plunge down another channel toward another sea. Thus the desert is crossed.

The desert is not replenished. Its life at a margin of life retains the condition of scarcity. The desert is barren, without fecundity, infertile, unarable, and fruitless. Desert creatures survive only through ingenious adaptation to austerity. In the desert, there is no fat. Cells secrete inward, since what is lost to the outside is forever lost. Solitude is this condition.

A kind of purity reigns. Mummies are preserved in their desert tombs for thousands of years. Metal will not rust, clay pots will not crumble. What is recorded of a past is not erased by the present. Time does not flow the same in the desert. When river, cloud, dew, and mist withhold contact, leaving life closer to death's cousin, sleep—inanimate and suspended, inward and aware—one is not touched in the usual way by tragic passions. What else but awareness survives the justice of elements unsupportive of life and that grind all tissue to mineral salt? The desert is not for nature but her opposite—consciousness. Its inhospitality to organic tissue at the same time is welcoming to a fine attention that arises from a Life within life. In its solitude lives a vision.

There is also the mirage. Rising like a heat shadow from over-heated earth, its illusory power encompasses eye and mind. Only a

129

body, when it tries to drink, is not fooled. Illusion finds a fit receptacle in human thirst. We are dry, so we readily believe the sight of water-hole, spring, or oasis on the next horizon. Ecstatic vision, like mirage, is a desert phenomenon. Desirous to drink at this source, people have wandered the sands, forsaking common sense, in search of it. Those of the desert warn gravely against it: "If you see a man by his own will climbing up into heaven, take him by the foot and throw him to the ground, because what he is doing is not good for him."

Survival is a matter of hoarding and planning. Ant or camel, cactus or scarab, each knows to accumulate for a future destined to have less than more. Adaptation requires a thick, inert crust to encase tender innards. Otherwise, vital substance is sucked out, leaving whitened shell and bones for the arid graveyard. The desert is where life returns to the core and is tested. It is sequestration, silence, and an interrogative brilliance of midnight's stars. It is where one learns discretion.

Where flow stops and drought begins may be anytime, anywhere—in the middle of a sentence, during toast or blessing or prayer, on a midday walk when powers are at their height, on waking. Wherever a barren stretches before us, the desert beckons. It is dryness about a heart, a certain parched quality of thought, a physical thirst quenchable by no known drink. One walks differently, as though sands underfoot were shifting and untrustworthy. A cairn, three stones haphazardly couched, point a direction, but which? Familiar bearings—projects, dreams, aspirations, achievements—are gone, an unmarked wilderness hems one in on all sides. In one's mouth, a taste of ashes, on one's blood, "an agony of flame that cannot singe a sleeve" (Yeats). Safety is not to be found in standing still.

The desert is an interval. It is a time of death and retrieval. Just as a droplet from the river becomes vapor, something must die on entering the desert's near edge if the far edge is to be neared. To cross is to be transformed. The desert is place of transformation.

What sustains a body, vessel of life's waters, on meeting this great everyday spirit? Only what one is able to carry in a leakproof container—and then, most lightly. Into an emptiness of desert sand one opens and pours an emptiness of self. Unconditional courage is required. To turn back in the crossing is to turn one's back on a summons to life. Alexander the Macedonian and his great army perished in refusing this vision. Alexander had pride, energy, power, and cunning. But he lacked a keen attention to the source of his provisions. As a result, scarcity fractured his legions, broke his men's will, and sucked his vitality away. Alexander died an ordinary death. Of what was he ignorant? Ammonas, a Desert Father, writes: "One man carries an axe all his life and never cuts down a tree. Another who knows how to cut gives a few swings and the tree is down. This axe is discretion." Had Alexander faced an interval of transformation squarely, a new life—of submission—rather than an old death—by conquest—would have been his.

It is to the unclouded sun that one must submit. When the river boils up to a cobalt sky, little remains concealed in summer's noon. Few shadows, scant underbrush, small variation in sand: One is less hidden and less able to hide. All movement must take the fact into account—a lizard's dart, an armadillo's lethargy, a scorpion's lightning stroke. Scorching light evokes a fear and trembling, for what cloaks one's nakedness? The first call of desert travel is presentness. Nostalgia may be fatal if it means loss of bearings, aimless wanderings, mirages, and delirium. To follow faint clues and secret markers is the way of crossing, to walk each step of the road. Though bright, uncompromising, and direct, this spirit speaks in subtleties. A broken palm frond, ants milling on their nest, a crease of shadow—its voice is almost inaudible, except in the sudden storm. A nomad's eyes, accustomed to the open, are unclouded by thoughts of home. They need no map in an uncharted land. They read the desert's vast impartial expression and travel in concert with it.

Though changeless, the desert is also in movement. Watch the fall of sand along a dune, the constant jockeying for position, the arc of gravity. Desert earth is no less static than the river. Currents, eddies, backwaters, and tides exist also in the desert. Verbs mark activity. As a verb, the desert is a process of abandon, a leaves-taking of attachments, a forsaking of an idea of life. One engages in the action by ceasing to live by stale habits. A disciple's desert is of his own making. He takes leave of a life already moribund to die there or to discover a new oasis. By forsaking his privilege as prince and courtier, Moses dwelt in the desert with those around him. He grew vigilant, watching a movement by which he deserted himself. Many not as active as he languished without their former comforts and hiding places. They could not leave. When they were hungry, manna fell from heaven, and they were fed; but a disquiet robbed them of a vision of the miracle. There was only deprivation and their unforsaken greed. They lived for a promise and a dream, oblivious to the holy place of their passage.

Even Moses could not enter fully into the desert. Magical signs and servitude to his God did not cleanse a stammering tongue. He who spoke with the divine could barely pronounce to the mortal. As chains of an invisible bondage were never burned off, his speech was unlike the desert air, clear. Though Moses knew magic and orchestrated miracles, the desert miracle—a return to an infancy of consciousness—forever eluded him. Because his entry was incomplete, Moses entered but failed to leave the desert. His death took him to the edge of the desert's far side, in sight of a holy land he would never inhabit. The laws of the desert are rigid. Be transformed, or endure your imperfection forever.

Jesus too knew the desert. Born to it though not of it, he tasted its scant joys and suffered its blinding question. A hand in benediction, a fragrance of dawn, an infant's babble, the laving of soap, a snake's scales, a rug pulled to the chin for sleeping, the moon—these he knew by rubbing up against life. And more: that the desert is a place of the chance event, that risk suspends known law, that directions suddenly reverse themselves, that patience and awe are precious things. He communed with the desert elements when they acceded to a divine spark and when they grew cold again in night frost. When he went to watch wind lift dust devils, who was able to watch with him? In the garden, his disciples were dreaming of homes far away. No one possessed his measure. Did he feel himself a desert—forsaken by the breath of life— when in death he cried, "Eloi, lama sabachthani?"

The desert, I have said, is absence and a confusion of trails. Seek a good guide, or better not to set foot in it at all—if one has choice. For often enough, the sands cover over human achievement. Whose cities lie beneath the dry seas of Egypt, Persia, and China? The desert travels where it will and manifests itself sometimes as a concentrated zone, sometimes as a diffuse nebula, a comet's tail. Unexpectedly, it may encircle and stare with phenomenal beauty at one's unreadiness at the center. A wasteland, its "dry sterile thunder without rain," (T. S. Eliot) looks in at us from all sides. The Fisher King is ailing. His fields lie fallow while famine walks the land—invisibily, even as tables groan under weight of empty serving bowls. Unaware, we inhabit, and are inhabited by, the desert. Its chant, "the cicada and dry grass singing," drones its warning in our ears. The Fisher King's disease consumes his body and mind until someone unbidden calls it to his attention. "What ails thee?" "How are you?" The desert is absence of relation and isolation. Unaware, we each wait alone in the desert for one whose care could guide rains to fall in a too, too parched heart.

But the desert has its flowerings. A cereus tends its bud for months and springs open at the stroke of midnight on a midsummer's eve to release a perfume delectable for miles. A yucca waits for every tenth year; a century plant, the hundredth. Patient husbandry is necessary to prevent early exhaustion. Yet blooms are barren, no insects come to pollinate them. Reproduction occurs by underground runners. Ingenuity, innovation, and the exceptional mark the way to continuation. The desert too is a flower, a barren brought forth by improvident flowerings of earth, overfrequent insemination, artificial fertility, quickened harvests, and restless breeding. Too full of ourselves, we have wanted more. Filled with ingenious schemes, we subdued earth and forced a perpetual spring—until exhaustion set in. Though the desert flowers on our waste heaps, unlike yucca it is not infertile.

Like salt, silica, and sulfur, a desert flower propagates by laws different from those of organic life. Crystalline, fragile, it is the product of an earthen cauldron. In unfamiliar places, crevices, ravine walls, splinters of rock, dry wells, such mineral flowers appear. When they seek at all, people seek their purity. It is written that a flower appears only to those who seek it in truth. In a lie, it turns invisible. This is a way of speaking of the test of truth. The solar furnace separates the coarse from the fine, leaving pure, refined stone as monument to its work. Such a work hides from one's hiding. The process is worthy of emulation. To a crucible, add the crude ores of fear, covetousness, and distraction; mix and compound. Set it to heat. After years, when separation of self commences, boil off the liquid in a closed retort. When tears become a white solid, take the new substance and begin the next phase. Such desert purification produces material capable of healing blindness and all mortal wounds. Use sparingly.

In desert places, eyes grow physically farther apart. Bedouin and hermit's look comes from being accustomed to gazing at the sky's rim, an infinite distance away. While they walk, stand in conference, sit by the camp fire, or lie under blazing stars, their eyes meet no impediment. Vision thereby stretches toward formlessness. The desert demands complete sacrifice of an old orientation. Perhaps Moses, having written the law, failed to be consumed by passion and stayed attached to the writing. Rilke writes,

> while a child's quite small we take it
> and turn it round and force it to look backwards
> at conformation.

(*Duino Elegies*)

This, our ordinary focus, sees past things to what we want done with them. We fail to greet the ailing king because of a preoccupying concern with our own self. Our eyes grow narrower and narrower. We leave off a call to cross but succumb to the desert in demeaning ways.

An unimpeded horizon works the inversion I speak of. As if a band that constrained the eyes suddenly snaps, focus opens up. What was nearest—ego's rapacious look—shrinks to a dot. What is farthest engulfs us, and we find ourselves turned round, immersed in "that pure, unsuperintended element one breathes" (Rilke). The sun's radiance is then a compass point, as is the scorching earth, the air searing the lungs, and a stillness echoing in the ears. The mirage of the wasteland vanishes. There is only sagebrush and the march of sand and a fragrance and flowering of Self that the desert brings forth.

What survives the desert interval is not what there dies its death. The first is behind, always behind, the other—until a transforming moment. The reversal is an advent that sets background foremost. Desert space has a different curvature. It is non-Euclidean. Lines meet the perimeter to emerge again in back of one's head. Parallels change their mind midway and coalesce to unity. Shadows do not obey their masters. What appears appears without premeditation. To forsake ordinary knowledge for an awe that catches the breath: This is desert survival.

20

MEASURE

A long the road, few companions are as faithful as one's walking stick. It is muscle. Light, strong, deft to the touch, it supports each step by adding to spring and lightening impact. It is an arm, warning of puddle, slick, and invisible depression long before the eye knows. It is implement, weapon, or gaming racquet, able to knock aside a stout rock without being damaged. Better its silent help than a foolish friend's, though it too places its demands.

To use the stick is also to engage in an action. The action is magical and unknown. A good stick is about the length of a good stride. If it is much longer, one is pulled along ahead of oneself and easily strains and tires. If it is too short, one feels hemmed in by the cramp of tendons working against themselves. Feet stumble, the breath falters, and the road grows bitter and long. Care is needed in choosing the stick, lest one's wish should weaken to follow the way whither it leadeth. Care reveals a secret action of the walking stick. It measures the stride and, by measuring the stride, measures the whole length of distance from here to there.

Measure is of a value as immense as it is invisible. Because its weight is less than a feather, we grow insensitive to its presence until, weighed down by its absence, we groan under its loss. This spirit is a great guide for us in any striving we wish to complete. With a subtle, unerring hand, measure keeps track of the aim and refuses to allow us to persist in our distractedness. Where we wander off a path, measure observes our state, calls us back, and reminds us of our inattentiveness.

Where we grow careless, it maintains our watch, preserves us from danger, and restores us to the direction of movement. Its effect is magical in how it quells the powers of an infirm, disquieted mind. Yet it never appears a sorcerer, choosing to direct its spells to the most unmagical and least suspecting of all partners, reason. Measure enchants thought, slows its frenetic pace, and persuades it to take notice of things. Thus does it bring thought to service.

Measure is a keeper of aim. It safeguards purpose from our reactions to distance and duration, thereby preserving initiative. This makes it a kind of memory, to which in root meanings it is related. Both retain experience in their possession, measure by encompassing a vision of the whole and with a charm bringing it down to the scale of the present. Dissipating powers of time and space are neutralized. That is magic, and the magic of measure is to relate a larger whole to *this* one.

How did measure come to its work? Measure is a work of hermetic craftiness. Recall the story of Hermes' famous theft. Just for a prank, he stole Apollo's prized herd. Apollo confronted Hermes and sought double damages, for the act was not only unfair but capricious. Laughing, the Trickster handed over his lyre in the name of justice. Apollo saw he was not cheated and was satisfied with the deal. He could then claim music as his own creation.

Thus is a mind forever enchanted with measure, which it takes to be its invention. This came about as a logical conclusion of the first incident. Apollo, lover of form, soon became enamoured of music. His skill won many a godly contest. He discovered that without rhythm and tempo, melody floats aimlessly aloft, having no effect on the ear and soul of things. Song that lacks movement is not song. That which gives impetus, keeps time, and sings is...measure. Since all song is of measure, Apollo quickly became god of both and with the eye of intellect, failed (as we fail) to see (as we will) that the bargain was a sorcery.

Measure was born from a trade of composition for impulsiveness, music for theft. The one is structure and language; the other, randomness and knavery. Hermes set the former equal, as compensation, to the latter. The balanced scales of compensatory justice were in fact first an expression of measure. But beneath solemn robes hides a musical joke! Listen. Measure makes unequals equal. It takes two impossibly different things—a stolen article and an invented form—and says they are the same. This is measure's sleight-of-hand, its enjoyment of absurdity, its hidden laughter. For at each enactment of measure, if we listen very carefully, there is Hermes laughing merrily in his cave.

All measure recapitulates the original hermetic bargain. Yet the enchantment of measure—making unequals equal—lies hidden behind the mask of reason. Measure resides in an equilibrating force, forever incommensurate with axioms of logic. Thus a logical point of view must have measure ultimately rest on absurdity. Such vision never peers beneath the surface. To look behind the mask is to notice that caliper and yardstick, calendar and milestone, sounding line and spectroscope, all partake of another kind of lawfulness. Such law, bane of a rational mind, is like Hermes' laugh—sudden to appear, swiftly penetrating, and unremitting.

Measure, magical maker of equations, like a traditional marriage broker, works in devious ways. Like her progenitor, she is not short on self-liking. (Some say the looking glass was invented by Hermes.) Measure divides a whole in order to represent herself to each part, thereby increasing her enjoyment. Such joy is truthful. For each part profits and is perfected by being measured and related to the whole. At every stride, the walking stick measures, and is measured by, the unbroken journey. Every stride passes over a unique parcel of ground, marked by its own configuration of earth, rock, plant, and tree. Every stride encompasses its unique blend of effort and momentum, ease and resistance. Yet utter difference is parceled out by measure into lengths equal in respect of being one and the same fraction of the whole measure. Then what is to keep parcels separate, once difference is obliterated? Forthwith, measure invents her most famous device—number. Number is measure's means of keeping track of the same thing without altering its sameness.

Numbers serve measure well. They are obedient to her call to equilibrate. They can be set equal each to each and yet remain distinct one from the other. They have long seemed magical, for they bedazzle the mind. As the natural expression of measure—the stick is six feet, the road is six miles—they speak, and we are charmed into believing their utter reliability. Much follows from this. Calculation and comparison, quantity and accuracy all derive from number. Thus devolve technology and the exact sciences. Because of number and measure that stand invisibly within it, we dare conceive of the cosmos as thoroughly knowable by a computational mind. From the great cosmos, lying beyond from where light has crept, to the miniscule cosmos, an atom of the atom, number tells the truth of things, unbent by the human eye.

If this were only truth! Just as we forget measure's magical origin while embracing a utility of exchange, we neglect also the deceptiveness of her speech. She cannot talk straight for long without betraying her pedigree. Pythagoras was first to notice this when he tried to compute the hypotenuse formed from the diagonal of a square. Pi, the ratio of the radius to the circumference of a circle, is also a famous example. Surds, irrationals, and incommensurables abound infinitely within number. They express a mathematical joke and give expression to the original hermetic impulse that set exactitude and arbitrariness equal.

We commonly suffer a common confusion. In many things, we mistake expression for voice. Many ways of taking measure—the measurements, inches, drams, bushels, acres—speak with the same silvery tongue and prevent us from being cheated in exchanges. A more egregious error (or deeper deception) in respect to measure is to confuse number with the equilibrating force itself. A walker then neglects how measure reveals her perfection in the stride and instead counts the number of strides needed to attain perfection. A sojourner neglects how measure enjoys portioning herself out equally and instead compares different portions. From this sort of amnesia comes the more and the less, the bettering and the aggravating, the preferred and the disdained. A measuring mind Protagoras the Sophist knew when he declared that "man is the measure of all things, of things that are that they are and of things that are not that they are not." Measure shrunk by so much becomes no more than measured, a deliberate, calculated action. The walking stick blind to a journey's divine destination is only a stick, useful but expendable.

When the spirit of measure is diminished, it returns to the bottle of the fable and is lost. The bottle lies hidden beneath the fern cover of an ancient beech tree. Stoppered away, measure no longer relates heaven to earth, earth to heaven, and "many ingenious lovely things are gone" (Yeats). While we languish in hunger, greed is unleashed. The reign of quantity proliferates diversity without end and bloats us with number. Mass production replicates the same, while real difference—the unique part receiving the measure of the whole—gets rubbed away. This is a belly that swells from malnourishment, not surfeit of plenty. A walker tries only to accumulate enough measured divisions of the road to finish the race. A vision of human destiny has vanished. One counts and the count wants only the next and the next. Thus does greed beget restlessness, and restlessness, insufficiency, and insufficiency, suffering, and suffering, hope.

When the cycle comes round again, hope is always of the fullness of the present moment. Dream—of riches waiting at the road's end or left long ago at home—departs, and we find ourselves on gritty soil beside a mountain stream where pure air burns the lungs and unfiltered light makes the eyes tear. A return of measure, or actually of ourselves, jolts the organism to openness. In a bottle's sudden unstoppering, time explodes the hourglass wherein the seconds are counted, while the moment's abrupt depth contains an actual eternity. Here, measure is distinguished from scale, since scale has to do only with relative size, and measure, with absolute relation. When we are ourselves, we know measure operates up and down the scale of creation, from the greatest to our own least to the least, and it is the voice of lawfulness. Sensing that, we are reunited with a summons that on all levels calls beings to join in the One Measure.

Ease and alertness belong to a walker's gait. Many steps lie between one rest and the next, and a mind tenses and wanders. When distracted, we mistake the walking stick's length for its measure. This is, as I said, due to a failure to listen. The clack-clack-clack of its tip gives a more accurate pronouncement of measure than does the stick's footage. A walk is a rhythm whose fit meter is a metronome, not a measuring rod. When measure—and not an uncompanionable stick—guides the step, tempo conveys a walker lightly forward. Feet find a cadence that relieves the strain of doing without one. One never tires when stick carries walker rather than walker the stick. Here again, measure's magic comes into play. The force to render unequals equal—the equilibrating force—replenishes vitality in equal measure to every moment. Regardless of difficulty, peril, treachery, or speed of stride, the force balances diverse claims on the attention by its inherent relatedness. Thus is a walk set in harmony with demands of the times, and a walker, one whose greatness consists in acting in time.

To continue on into the night is pleasant. After songbirds quiet, a full moon lights the way, lending color and visibility as if to things of a dream. Silence calls forth an interior dimension. The light shows the otherness, each from each, of things. One walks unfamiliarly as though in a lunar landscape, muscles and skeleton related differently to an impulse to move. Uncanniness envelops each stride. Measure is therein returned to its primitive setting, for originally the moon (*mene*, in Greek) took the measure of all things. From the moon's cycle came the month (*mens*), and from the month the implements of everyday value. The moon's twenty-seven phases represent regular and consistent change. Until the return on the twenty-eighth, the sequence lacks cyclicity. The cycle becomes a cycle only when the moon is again full.

In luminous dark, we see a shadow of fullness joined to the new crescent. It reminds us of the moon's measure—a complete cycle. In completion of the cycle resides the act of measure.

A cycle is also a return. Only change that involves a return, like the moon's, is cyclic. Thus, to measure, in the moon's terms, implies a return—to fullness. Ancient astronomers who based all measure on the moon had profound insight into the nature of this everyday spirit. The action of measure—the equilibration of unequals, whatever sort they are—returns a walker to wholeness. The advent of measure is a shock. In its wake one remembers oneself and that one did not remember. Absence healed, amnesia cured, hope restored, walker walks in his own shoes and feels how they pinch his feet. Gravel is sharp, leaves are smooth. His moon-shadow walks to one side.

On the journey, the local respects the cosmic in a simple, direct fashion. Starlight plays off night dew, and the sun falls equally on things. The note of a sparrow orients the compass and opens a heart. When one listens while walking, the return to measure is double. It returns one to oneself *and* to a greater totality. In its magical equilibration that sets incomparables together as equals, measure puts a human being in the equation whose other side is all and everything. Whence derives a bold, daring ploy, to place a fleck of dust beside the sun and speak of their mutual comprehension? What could measure mean? How can the flame of gaseous nebulae be compared to a heart's steadfast flame?

The way things are on our own level is familiar, while on other levels, as in a moonscape, they are not often grasped. This pertains to how we escape our measure even as we lack it. For as starlight is reflected in dew, so too is a bedewed surface of grass mirrored in stars. A keenness required to witness such reciprocity is rare, as rare as the full advent of measure. But it exists. The finding of one's measure reverberates on all scales throughout the cosmos. The totality is increased and made happy by the discovery. An energy bestowed on life is returned to its source. A great, great cycle is thereby completed, the downward is balanced by the upward. In abundance, all creatures breathe freely and are joined together in an exclamatory moment. In that joining, the cosmos is renewed. Such is nothing other than an exultation by the breath of measure.

21

THE BOWL

The bowl has the look of waiting. When it is empty, waiting is its perfection, for the bowl was made to hold that which cannot hold itself. The bowl is a hand, cupped upward toward the rain. Falling, the rain has nowhere to go and, so, cannot be detained save by supplication. All bowls imitate human hand gesture, palm concave and stretched toward a generosity of heaven. A hand so gestured does not wait *for* anything. Its shape and time *is* waiting. So too with the bowl. The bowl is for praying.

When full, the bowl is still for waiting. Brimming with rain after a passing shower, the bowl is there to catch sun and magnify its exuberance. For jay, thrush, and sparrow, the bowl waits on their thirst. It exemplifies the law of service. One thing serves another that serves a third that, in the round-robin exchange, supports the first. Or in shade, discarded, the bowl waits for sky to breathe in its water and end a drought that parches earth. Even when full, the bowl attains its perfection, since it waits empty of expection, dream, and confusion.

A whole night Siddhartha sat beneath the bo tree in the garden. Unable to contain itself, heaven rained in abundance. Yet human life was parched, and men and women suffered alone in their pettiness and defeat. Waters of life fell but quenched no one. How to comprehend the contradiction? Siddhartha had for years thought the problem was self-indulgence. One needed to master stoicism, austerity, and ascesis. Yet mastery of denial only strengthened the poison. It embittered the mind and weakened the body to the degree that the palms no longer lifted upward. Muscles stiffened into fists and clutched at whatever fell near. No one could catch the rain that way. Siddhartha's thirst grew immense yet he continued to refuse the body's own gesture. Finally, after holding his breath too long, a paroxysm of release worked its way out. When he rejoined humanity, he understood his lack. No bowl had stood ready.

The recognition was magical. At that very moment (the story goes), a young woman who had beheld Siddhartha's vigil came to the garden. She bore a portion of sweet rice—rice cooked in sweetened milk—in a bowl. It was for the one who had rent the veil of illusion. Its advent marked his return.

Slowly, like a lumbering sea creature, recognition goes over to action. Tension has dissolved, movement is liquid. What contains it now? The senses awaken to an outer world. Dappled sunlight through the pipal leaves, dry earth beneath, a mourning dove aloft, and an ambrosiac aroma like "a solace of ripe plums seeming to fill the air" (W.C. Williams). He holds the bowl of sweetened rice in his hand. It fits perfectly. A single grain finds its way to his mouth. Hunger as such is recognized. Fullness is about to replace emptiness, and emptiness, fullness. The gesture gives expression to realization, and Siddhartha becomes the Buddha, the Empty One.

Silence does not contain the bowl, nor the bowl silence. Though it waits, the bowl does not do so mutely. Listen. Empty or not, the bowl is full of sound, always. A summer breeze breathes, gently. Every bowl, no matter what its construction, is a singing bowl such as Tibetans make out of silver-brass alloy. Circle the rim at the right velocity with a stick, and an uncanny sourceless drone fills space. Sound comes from everywhere to saturate each point. Direction as ordinarily known is destroyed in the manner in which Joshua destroyed the walls of Jericho. The singing leaves one elsewhere, separate from usual preoccupations that place one somewhere.

The bowl, however, must be approached with sensitivity. Too much speed or pressure on the stick produces degenerate noise. The bowl measures one's poise. Not to try too hard. Right touch leaves mind clear and body alert. That the bowl, stirred and warmed by the stick, sings with such voice reveals the bowl for what it is—a diaphragm that is lifted ever so slightly before it is let fall. It has a thin skin, of metal, earth, or wood, that responds quickly to each change.

Of any construction, a bowl resonates when touched. That is because the bowl, never mute or silent, is predominantly a vessel for voice. It is a chamber of a certain thickness that resounds to the air it holds. Air is its emptiness. The bowl is also a tympan. An invisible membrane imparts feel, texture, and resistance to emerging sound. Constantly filled with air, the bowl is consistently vocal. The bowl at all times practices voice. Sound is also the bowl's perfection.

A drum is an inverted cousin of the bowl, with a skin specially stretched over the resident air to amplify sound. But a tympanic membrane does not change the essence of the bowl. It creates volume, no more. It exploits an essential property for the sake of enjoying the bowl even more. A percussionist is not the only one to do this. Invert the design by a bit—make the bowl less rigid—and you have a diaphragm, the bowl whose shape controls breath and voice. Placed below lungs and larynx, the bowl has power great enough to regulate a flow of air in and out of our human dwelling place. It's power also is great enough to speak with intelligence. To flex the bowl is to change the sound that escapes its lips into the ears of the world. The bowl is sensitive enough to resound to a brain's summons and render audible the inaudible.

Gold beaten into the shape of a bowl is a new sun. A parabolic mirror, it catches light and hurls it back to a central focus. The spectacle speaks to the bowl's destiny. But it disguises the origin. Bowls are of humble earth and properly made of earthen substance. To make a bowl, take a lump of moist clay. Round it to a ball and warm it in your hands. With a thumb, press in to form a hole, and, starting from the bottom, press out from the inside. Move in a circle, always in the same direction. As the walls thin, a mouth will open. Continue without trying to shape the process. When the rim is satisfactory, flatten the underside to create a stable seat. Let dry.

After firing, such a bowl fits in the hands while one is sitting and is part of the body. To the Buddha, it seemed this way upon tasting the sweet rice. The bowl was his body, and his body was the bowl. Thus he discovered an important fact—the bowl is a measure. When at rest, one is a bowl, and one's body looks like a bowl, inverted. Bowl and body both are containers. As the bowl contains air, body contains a subtly breathing energy. Upon listening, one can hear it say "I am."

Making a bowl is practice for making a human, as the word suggests. This is a practice no human has ever completed. One-half of our dual origin derives from the Potter's skill that formed us from clay and poured life in. We are "made of humus," earthborn, of the ground. The mortal, perishable aspect is subject to laws that the bowl is subject to. It can sing, sit, breathe, hold food, be full or empty. Is there a difference? If there is, it concerns an intention breathed into us. That intention permeates every being, bowl, beast, and human, but in nature our relation to it is special. Bowls, things we make, know the fact better than we. Rilke says that they

Want us to change them entirely, within our invisible hearts, into—oh, endlessly—into ourselves! Whosoever we are.

We alone on earth are able to transform coarser substances to finer, distill an essence of experience, and return it to the source. The potter, exhausted by building the bowl, is replenished by her enjoyment of it. So, too, that who made earth and all that is made of earth is replenished by human awareness, the emptiness of the bowl. That stillness contains an echo of original intention—or the intention itself—and rejuvenates the Maker. Just as one's burden lightens when a weighty purpose is held in common, so too He who hears his work taken up by others is restored to firmness. The bowl supports the potter.

Under a tree, the bowl waits, complete save for a use. It has caught rain to fullness and been emptied again by drought. Never mute, it has sung many songs. Now it stands upright on a leg, mouth open to heaven. Its posture expresses a vocation true to the nature of this most composed of everyday spirits. The posture belongs to a beggar.

A beggar squats, sits, leans, or stands by the roadside. A traveler himself, he waits to meet others who travel. Though he may address someone ("Spare some change?" "Bakshis," "S'il vous plaît"), the palm is his voice. Outstretched upward, it entreats heaven to speak mercifully though the gold of a chance pilgrim. An impulse to fill what is empty is powerful. In times when greed does not predominate, a beggar is given an honored place. His presence is a reminder. Those who pass also proceed, mouth open heavenward, and unknowingly beg the bread of succor and restoration.

A mendicant displays his poverty. The image calls up strong feelings, often a refusal to take him in. Shame rises in us, and we try to hide our face. Who now does not meet a beggar full of reaction and dread? We who hurry on have traded our poverty for riches. We own clothes, provisions, books, memories, dreams, and...ourselves. We have much that we could give in response to his entreaty. He has relinquished ownership to affirm his empty bowl. His poverty reflects a double image back to us, an image of a double denial. We deny we have alms to give and that we too seek alms. Thus we are not detained by his neediness nor by our own.

In his simple, sparse, or shabby dress, a beggar awaits resources of fellow travelers. They hurry on, burdened by a dilemma he has resolved—to be free from attachment. By a vow (of a monastic order), choice, or circumstance, he has agreed to accept what is given him and to lead a life based on it. With no past or future, he is turned wholly toward his bowl, toward that which serves it. He who has no other profit profits from what we yield to him, of our excess or even of our due share. When we come with a willingness to meet his condition, we too know a freedom.

Beggar and bowl, when we allow ourselves to be greeted, have a look about them. This one is forthright, that one reticent, the other inquiring or apologetic or prideful. But all wait upon their station without names. A beggar is anonymous. Though a beggar may be known well, his power of surrender makes him transparent. He is less hidden, as are we when we enter into a moment of giving over, and thus can dwell in a public place. Unnamed, he is no longer clothed with a name and shows himself nakedly for what he is. Through the bowl, the beggar has learned the root impulse to attachment—the name. To call a thing by its name is to wrench it from a formless background. Control, domination, utility, and ownership all follow from a grasp on the name. To adopt a quiet, waiting posture is to allow the grasp to loosen, the name to be forgotten. It is to become a profitable servant.

The bowl receives what passersby give it. It is empty, so it receives a gift without naming it. Its spirit is apparent in its nonattachment. A beggar—also without name—is sustained by the bowl's contents. Bread, oranges, dates, money nourish a body. That is necessary, but alms are what he in essence awaits. Charity does not always deposit a gift with the bowl. We in passing by are often distracted by guilt and worry. The gift then is not of a mind's heart that sings with the bowl's song, but of its fear that wishes to mute it. Its sustenance is crude and begrudging, the way a mocking, arrogant song can be.

Uncharitable ways run deep. When we give because we feel a beggar's deprivation, we still fail to give alms. Empty, the bowl is deprived of no thing. Full, its deprivation has not been relieved. The bowl does not ask charity to make up for something lacking—though what is offered is gratefully accepted. Compassion is recognition of the bowl's emptiness. Then there is no difference between the bowl, what it solicits, and what it gets. To see the bowl, how it stands on earth, how it catches sunlight and rain, how it waits, itself calls forth a response. In midstride, one stops. The wind breathes, and the lungs. A memory—like that of a spring day—returns, and with it remembrance of a larger life in which one participates. The giving of self to Self lies in the inspiration of the bowl. One takes it in and fills it with like kind in return.

A beggar—keeper of the bowl—holds a great challenge. To him one must give away that which occludes reality from the eyes. That is the gift the empty bowl desires. Yet one prizes it above all else, for it is one's suffering, whatever else it is called. To make oneself miserable is to devour compassion near its source. Thus we all are made beggars. Pain and one's true response to it remain unfelt when aversion to pain preoccupies the mind. Thought then is of avoidance, of a disguised encounter, of false sentiment, of nostalgia. What is called "happy" is a false smile.

The empty bowl asks for this secret pain, the pain of pain, that hides unto nakedness. When a beggar's stance stops us, to return us to an unlearned pang of existence, then we are able to lay much down in charity. The empty bowl is compassionately filled and remains without content. We are emptied of our fool's gold and greatly gladdened by that. The bowl holds our happiness which, while we ourselves held it, was our suffering. Our smile is like the Buddha's, the wind uplifting the lips.

The bowl was the first thing to meet the Buddha's eyes after he emerged from the immutable realm. How the bowl spirited his mind from formlessness to its simple form is a secret the bowl does not share. A preestablished harmony must have existed. The young woman set the bowl beside the bo tree. The bowl bore food to be eaten. It waited. The Buddha, bearing knowledge, weary but gladdened, took the food and left the bowl empty. In this way, the bowl became a first transmission of knowledge of the other shore. Thereafter, it was possible to take up the bowl and by that act become an initiate.

Yet like all compassionate spirits, the bowl disguises its wisdom. It puts on a mask. Commonplace, lowly, and nameless, it patiently sits on a shelf awaiting the hand that, in imitation of a bowl, will cradle it. Contact with a shell of earth is the way of meeting the spirit whose everyday home lies within. A caring touch immediately throws one open to the being who touches and, through this gate, to the entire cosmos. Then, what one holds—the bowl—has an origin that points in a direction. In that direction lies what one is here for.

PART FOUR

LAO TZU

22

INK

You could tell he was going out into the desert. That was his end, from which no man could dissuade him. The only hope was to slow and divert the intention, for a moment, to allow it to bestow its gift of understanding.

The man was world-weary and heartsick. But that part was disguise, as was his shabby dress and bent walking stick. When you looked, the step sprang back up without pressing in on earth. If you touched him, an electric bolt shot through your arm. One glance from his eye, and your mind stopped.

Who would detain him? Few noticed, and fewer dared. Through the frontier town, a window to endless sands, he passed without leaving a mark. At the caravansary, he had tea and his simple meals. With shopkeepers, there were simple dealings, an inquiry after herbs, a disposal of coins, a purchase of new sandals. With him no one spoke, though he did not go in silence.

Finally, twilight came. In the long desert twilight, many things change round, but not his resolve. At a first star, he entered the gatekeeper's hut. According to law, he required one last permit.

A form was ready, but for the ink. The gatekeeper went to his desk and started to rub the ink stick against the bowl. It slowly darkened the water. Again and again, he repeated the circle. Never had the liquid turned so jet black, black as obsidian. The candle did not reflect in it. A purpose firmed in him. He looked the man in the eye.

"Before you go," he said, "there is one question."

149

"Yes?" said the other.

"Why is ink dark?"

With rice cakes and rum, the other took pen one last time and wrote through the night. As everyone slept, stars wheeled around heaven. At dawn, he was gone.

A pool of ink lacks form. Expressing chance or mindless nature, it sits on white paper, a blot. Slowly as it spreads, part sinks into the pores and is sucked into the air, lofted by a summer breeze. Dried, the other part takes shape, gaining no form but permanence. It no longer moves in an image of change. The image is removed as ink becomes fixed where the pool had been. The immutable realm—that which is always here—is formless and is in constant flux. Ink that cannot help but serve formlessness now serves the immutable in a different way, as record, chronicle, or history. It tells what became of the pool.

When liquid ink dries, it leaves its mark. Ink is a suspension of very fine, opaque, insoluble particles that become a residue as soon as the liquid evaporates. The particles never settle in a stoppered bottle or shallow well. Freed to thin or broad strokes of a brush or pen, ink returns to its original, unmixed condition. This expression of its inky nature tells much concerning a transformation of state.

Keen eyes are needed to mark a transition from inkpot to inked line. Even though each sign, glyph, cipher, symbol, or letter is contained in an ink bottle, who is master of the fluid's legibility—if not the one who picks up implement and inks? How does ink make secrets manifest within its dark vortex? To whom? To read the ledger while ink still flows requires a memory of the present. To follow an emergent need, to fill freely a shape of response, to keep a faithful record of that which expresses itself: A reader must heed qualities of formlessness. These are eyes of discernment that see "where time is shrivelled down to time's seed corn" (Pound, "The Flame"). A constancy lives in their gaze. They are with nib or quill as it breaks the ink's surface, is called to the substance, conveys it to paper, and applies it. They do not dictate, but take dictation from ink. Their sharp edge is a patient heart. Only to these eyes is the magical spirit of ink coaxed to appear.

Other eyes are made for form. They find focus in definition, contour, and shape. They read only the written word. These are eyes of forgetfulness. They narrow in concentration to seize ink's power and purvey it for a private purpose. Then the ink produces a human device, no more. Writing—the drying of the ink—is the invention.

About writing, tradition warns of danger. To Ammon, king of Egypt, came Troth, the clever one, puffed up with inventiveness. He brought ink and began to write on some papyrus. He made ciphers full of meaning. They recorded events and happenings in a way that gave an illusion of time standing still. It would, he argued, be a great boon to humans. Unimpressed, Ammon admonished him. "If men learn this," he said,

> it will implant forgetfulness in their souls; they will cease to exercise memory because they rely on that which is written, calling things to remembrance no longer from within themselves, but by means of external marks. (*Phaedrus* 275a)

Before this time, precedence was given to the transient realm between heaven and earth. This was an age of purity, when the immutable was in love with playthings of change. Things looked for "rescue through something in us, the most fleeting of all" (Rilke). The deep, opaque pool from which things arose to blossom in the light of memory was respected. From its inky depths were gathered all that could be kept in the human dwelling—which was everything. In a vibrancy of remembrance, things found a home, not in changelessness but in recurrence. Then there was invention, of skill and contrivance, often by theft and always at a great cost. Inventor fell in love with device. A pandemic forgetfulness spread over humankind. A keen vigil from on shore gave way to a darting glance. By chance, the eye fell on certain markings. They were Troth's gift.

The gift breeds an indolence inasmuch as it dispenses with a specific demand—for one's presence. Eyes are able to meander over signs without leaving off the dream. To read, a mind uses a code or calculus, not remembering itself. The essence of reality—its very transience—becomes veiled behind ciphers. The while that one fears impermanence as loss, a love of hiding grows, wherein "the mortal does all it can to put on immortality" (*Symposium* 207d). This is the stance of our age. It is of the alphabet, grammar, and writing, dictionaries, encyclopedias, and libraries. To read *about* things dispenses with a need to exercise recollection, to engage an action of mind, to journey from oblivion to knowledge. The inkwell holds a supreme pragmatic value: to keep thought from passing away. Mind itself is grown flaccid.

Ink, I have said, leaves a trace on drying. The trace allures. It is darkness within darkness, a stick with two ends, both danger and promise. Therein dwells this adventuresome spirit. The peril is a mind's confusion, a promise to come "back to the source where even names cease" (Valery, "The Rower"). A disciplined hand unerringly picks the right end. What is its discipline? Before entering the desert sand that one night, the man wrote, "If nothing is done, then all will be well." The discipline is to let be.

We too leave traces. Action draws forth a stroke from the inkwell and makes a mark upon the world. One line calls another to it, a meshwork of consequences. The intricacy catches our attention. Days are spent deciding how to leave a special trace. Here the presiding spirit is that of ink. Who can use ink while not lost in daydreams of what will be written? Who can watch how the pool never dries?

That skill is unlearned and must be unlearned again after so much worldly writing. In autumn, on a hillside with the sharp smell of oak, shouts of small boys. They have been surprised by a stand of pokeweed, its sacred inkberry ripened by night frosts. Branched like candelabras, pokeweed stalks are purple-veined and turgid with juice. Each is crowned with a cluster of berries of as deep a purple as nature provides. In afternoon sun, the berries bend lustrous and full. No one eats of the pokeberry and lives to tell the effects of its potent toxin. But the boys know the lore and harvest them for another end. It is ink they seek.

Break clusters off. Thick stalks are strangely delicate to the touch. Find a flat rock, one with a shallow depression. Get a fat stick for a mallet, and crush the berries. Push pulp to one side. Let inkberry juice collect into a pool deeper and darker than the imagination. Even the sun that brightens the whole earth cannot penetrate the surface to leave a shadow. Gather the power of that pool. Now quickly find a stem of yarrow or aster and something to write on—white birch bark is best. What marks you make do not matter, a note home, a letter to a secret love, a treasure map. They are indelible.

Which brings to mind invisible ink. Its pool is transparent and hides nothing beneath its surface. Hence traces are hidden, the way air is, until one knows how to look. Juice of an ordinary lemon possesses such properties. As one writes, one apparently writes nothing. A page is as blank after as before. But take the paper and hold it aloft above a candle flame. By a secret process, heat induces the signs to come out of concealment. Losing their shyness, they slowly disclose themselves. Form revealed, they are stayed until a mind frees them up to contemplation and sends them on their journey. The message appears!

All blankness that meets the eye too holds tracings of hidden pools. Earth has borne beings familiar with the ink spirit who have dipped quill into well and written. Nature contains numerous pages that together constitute the book of knowledge. By what unknown refinement is their script brought forth? The heat of attention renders visible what already is invisibly there. The prose of the world, composed in invisible ink, becomes legible only to a faithful reader. Her fidelity is to a still pool, its surface ripples, a secret flower of its depths, and to the timing. To watch for the Self in the pool of self is like discovering pokeberry. Tripping over a hillside, the wanderer is suddenly face to face with "beauty's very self." Opened from the inside, perception is one with its hunger for impressions. Avidity is the condition of reading. The rest is a mind's dissection.

Ink, as I said, is impartial. It is destroyer or creator of meaning, a haphazard blotch that spoils a page or a shape rife with hidden import. It is a nullity or an opening to another reality. The difference is a matter of aim. A cuttlefish gives us a precise example. It survives predators' pursuit by means of ink. Sepia jets out and envelopes friend, enemy, and self alike when anxiety attacks. Contours lose definition, place disappears, and the familiar is cast into darkness. An act of beclouding the waters is *Sepia*'s exercise of will. Ink erases sight and allows for escape. In much of our hiding we imitate a cuttlefish, master of this aspect of the spirit. Inking over allows us to avoid the unavoidable. Escaping, however, we come up short. That which we lose sight of is ourselves.

Keeping brush pointed, well black, and hand steady, one serves ink in a different way. The station is to remain poised on the edge of the pool. Ancient Chinese practitioners of the brush stroke knew to dip from where ink is blackest. The edge is the frontier—ink changes to not-ink and back again. To come to the edge is to be related to what is constant amidst change. Looking carefully with feet on the ground, you can see sky mirrored in dark liquid. As clouds scud across a mountain top—of both heaven and image of heaven—the movement contrasts with the solidity of the shore's edge. To watch, even as surface is broken by drawing forth ink, demands a sharpness that lines never possess. Herein resides poise. Without interfering, poise awaits a time to break upon the pool. It does not quit when depth appears. Poise remains on the edge. The edge is where form is called to existence.

Ink forms—brush, nib, or felt tip—derive importance from their origin. They point to formlessness, even as a road sign points to one's destination. But we cannot reckon the incommensurability of the two worlds—even in wonders drawn from the inkwell. Thus intelligence expresses intimacy, though at the same time it risks indiscretion. Not knowing the way between, we cannot but fail to calculate the gap joining heaven and earth. We confound our invention—that line of ink— with its aim—to merge with a blank sheet it marks.

That we are beset with confusion is not entirely our doing. Ink surrounds itself with a murkiness with regard to its origin. When the motion of things is obscure in its beginning, clarity becomes impossible. Pool or well may be an imitation of a still-earlier appearance of the spirit. Since only a trace of earlier times remains, much needs to be inferred. The action of ink is to dry, its state, a liquid. As an ink master knows, ink is made with water. The word, however, suggests otherwise, coming through the Greek *enkaustos*, "burnt" (*kaustos*) + "in" (*en*). Fire inevitably leaves markings on a cave wall, the sacrificial altar, or stones surrounding the fire pit. Some have a special shape. Attention is inevitably drawn to commune with the markings. They seem signs fraught with meaning, signifying something they are not, bearing import from beyond themselves. What produces them? What do they portend?

The use of ink begins as a study of fire markings. In each cipher is a deposit that vibrates with an energy of fire. "I knew not words but wrote with the quickness of fire," Boehme said. Great intelligence, speed, and decisiveness mark the movement of fire. Whatever enters a whirlwind of combustion is transformed. Wood and paper turn to ash, ore to metal, earth to salt. The black carbon mark left on a ceramic bowl after firing is a record of transformation. It holds a power to evoke the same in its reader. For those who seek passage through the transitional realm, a record is invaluable. Such marks are divinatory, prophetic, and sacred.

Ink copies fire markings. Ink was initially made by pulverizing burnt charcoal and adding it to water. The black pool was thus invented. Let the suspension dry, and the work of fire reappears. That the work is work once removed is the essential work of ink. Ink duplicates reality and participates in it by duplication. By means of ink, chronicles are kept and the hand of time—moved by fire—momentarily stayed.

23

THE LAUGH

The laugh rises to the top. It is a bubble driven heavenward by a physics of effervescence, not to be denied by all obstacles of gravity. Neither misfortune, sorrow, tears, nor pain slows it for long, for the laugh is light and in an upward direction seeks the being of light. It rises to the occasion, any occasion, even death.

From over a crest of the hill, from the glen, comes the sound of children at play. Shrieks and shouts, ballyhoos and singsongs, are ambiguous with respect to suffering or joy. They are loudest of sounds, but do not say whether concord or discord rules the hour. Only with closer listening do sounds—"hidden excitedly, containing laughter" (Eliot)—resolve the question. The laugh is conferred by harmony, and its spirit is of relatedness and ease. All sides are brought back to balance by laughter that rises like a carnival tent over the treetops.

The laugh suffers a great many impersonations that becloud a simplicity of spirit. Each appropriates the laugh and qualifies its unconditional freedom for a limited end. Cruel and taunting laughter, mocking and derisive laughter, forced and contrived laughter, bestial and tormented laughter, precious and lewd laughter—all strive to make use of choiceless ease. The laugh, when pure, completely pierces a crust of ego. Below the stiffness, what has no use determines the course of things and enables use of this or that. Like a subterranean fountain, the laugh that emerges in sunlight is subject to conditions of the depths. It can be controlled according to fashion but never without revealing its unfashionable origin. Its unlearned note, moreover,

155

can be learned—that is, copied—to produce effects of fear, anxiety, doubt, greed, hesitancy, the whole scale of human emotional life. To sing a song of the laugh is quite different from being sung by it. A child knows the difference.

Of the everyday spirits, the laugh is unique in being an *arche*-sound. Two other *arche*-sounds are the word one calls oneself by—*I*—and *Om*, "That syllable indeed is the supreme" (*Katha Upanisad* 2.16). The three together divide and exhaust a ground of being, in the way the good, the true, and the beautiful do. *Om* expresses goodness, *I*, truth, while we, hearing strains of laughter rippling an evening calm, know the laugh as beauty itself. Such sounds are uncreated. They issue forth from wholeness like sympathetic vibration does from a tuning fork. Each is a smaller whole resounding in like pitch with the greater whole. Each has a power of evoking the same sound in another. We are unsurprised at the contagiousness of the laugh. We are, however, astonished at how the laugh transmutes repulsive, ugly, loathsome, or ungainly looks to beauty. As a forbidding mask drops, the grace of unpretentious laughter opens the eyes to what waits excitedly hidden.

A bubble of joy, the laugh rises to the top "like the bloom of youth does on those in the flower of their age" (Aristotle, *Nicomachean Ethics* 1174b.33). It lives in its own time, and when it comes, it stays the moment a little while. In the fairy tale, all who tried were unable to make the dour princess laugh. Only when she by chance saw a fool who carried his donkey on his back did she burst (like a bubble) into laughter. Ice melted, and levity easily escaped into the atmosphere. Means exist, moreover, by which to prod, poke, tickle, and eventually prick the skin into a laugh. They also serve this dynamic spirit in the way in which a cultivated rose serves the same beauty as a wild one, but differently. Approaches to laughter are three: intoxicants, jokes, and comedy.

Wine returns one to unpretentiousness. The grape is of earth and like many earthly things has a tender pulp protected by a tough skin. When they are fermented together, one grape is no longer separate from another. Together, their substance is transformed. The action of wine on a psyche is analogous. Integument softens and grows permeable. As one's boundaries—limits of a pretender's domain—are no longer sharply defined, one blends more easily with an element that all have in common. Communication expands beyond a narrow, pent-up, mental channel to embrace organic feeling, including a feel for wholeness. In a Dionysiac or bacchanal, release is often explosive, possessing

an effervescent force of the grape fermented in the bottle. Into the
melee, the laugh escapes.

No longer pretending to be different, one joins together in
laughter. Riotous, inarticulate, sexual, the laugh of revelry returns one
to a natural past in which impulse and instinct command action. Such
a wholehearted surrender to absurdity cleanses a mind and sensitizes it
to forces beyond human dwelling. The risk is great. Vision can pierce
the skin of things and swell to cosmic proportion. Ecstasy, however,
may lead to a rapture that abjures the acid soil from which the grape
grows. Then mind is possessed—or dispossessed of its ground. Excess
and frenzy may fill a void left by temperance. An encounter with energies of the intermediate realm may prove fatal. One could die in a mad
fit of laughter.

Still, wine need not abandon balance but might weigh things
more urgently. Sobriety then yields to, as Alcibiades says, "philosophical frenzy" or "sacred rage" (*Symposium* 218b). Temperance ceases to
hide truth behind measured phrases. In the openness, the laugh takes
in one's own idiocy. A bubble of conceit pops. Bang! Or, in Alcibiades' image, a paper satyr (an ancient form of the piñata) bursts and
spills its penny contents. In the wake rise real questions. What attitude
to have toward the stupor encasing one's life? Whence the impulse to
meet one's destiny? How to traverse the space between heaven and
earth? As laughter precedes interrogation, it must follow it. When
laughter dies, one takes oneself too seriously. An inner beauty—the
source of the outer—is forsaken for a mind's vanity. Thus Alcibiades
asks, "Are you asleep, Socrates?" "No, I'm not," comes the answer
(*Symposium* 218c).

Which brings up the joke. Wine provokes the laugh by unstiffen-
ing the carriage of ourselves and revealing our graceless, pompous,
hysterical manner. It is a lubricant of earth and reinjects an earthiness
into our flights of fancy. Its effect is organic. The intoxicated laugh
takes one to midregions between shores before succumbing to inebri-
ation. A good joke, by contrast, works on a mind, since it conveys the
fact of timeless intelligence. "Eternity is just time enough for a joke"
(Hesse). Logic steers mutable mind. It directs thinking along timeworn channels, lest thought get other ideas and wander distracted into
the unknown. It thereby safeguards soundness, sanity, and sobriety.
The joke is a rebel against convention. It is daring, daunting, and
dashing to cherished ideals. Its content is the same no matter what its
disguise. It is a perception of contradiction. Logic asserts that some-

thing and its negation cannot both coexist. The joke says, they do, and by the way, they're in you. By our contradictions are we known. They expose us, lies exploded, fakery thrown to the wind, air let out of the balloon. Helium going skyward is none other than laughter, traversing the region toward the sun.

Put more geometrically, the joke is a recognition of incongruity. The right hand is in the wrong glove, or the shoe that is supposed to fit does not. The road curved left while the convoy went straight, straight into a quagmire. The disagreement is between mind and reality. The two cannot be made to correspond. The joke turns on our insistence that we are right, no matter what the facts are. In its clearer light, our very limitations, dissolved, reveal the way to greater freedom.

> Mulla Nasr Eddin's friend wanted to borrow his clothesline. "Sorry," said the Mulla. "I'm using it. To dry salt." "How's it possible to dry salt on a clothesline?" "It's easy when you don't want to lend it."

> The watchman caught Nasr Eddin prying up the window of his own house at midnight. "What are you doing, Mulla?" he asked. "Locked out?" "Shhh. People say I sleepwalk. I'm trying to surprise myself and find out."

The joke brings the laugh by revealing our laughable attempts at reason. That is the joke's mission, and it is taken most seriously. Surprisingly, by voice and posture, the joke is akin to a beggar. The original Sanskrit word for *joke* means "he implores." The joke begs our attention for a moment, this moment, to remind us of a gap in our logic. Calculation again has fallen shy of the mark, deduction is flawed, and (by the way) the choice of means was horrendous. The joke beseeches that we stop. The situation needs another look. Our eyes are trained too narrowly. The joke prays we forget our self-importance. We have taken hold of an idea of who we are, from which all reasons follow. To release our hold, it offers us release to the laugh.

The joke begs our alms whose coin is laughter—silvery, throaty, or visceral. With comedy, third provocateur of the laugh, we pay in a different way. Witness to a theatrical drama, we are shown a humorous edge to things. The edge cuts to the quick with trenchant satire, sarcasm, and irony. Human folly thus dissected by ridicule or scorn is seen to be what it is—a weakness that can be made into strength. We are invited to laugh because we are transparently not what we seem to be. Laughter, in rising, separates us from ourselves. A joy of nonattachment restores resolve. In the laugh is consciousness of humanity and of that from which humanity springs. Great is comedy's means of evoking the *arche*-sound, and great is the laugh's power to lead us across the intermediate realm.

A laugh begins in silence before taking off as an audible vibration. But what of the laugh that never grows audible? The one that stays so close to the ground that it blends perfectly with other sounds of earth? Then we have the smile, a soundless laugh. The smile is itself a miracle. Both words stem from a common root, the Latin *mirari* (to wonder at). Filled with wonder, one is emptied of preoccupation. Struck by astonishment, one stops perceiving through expectations and confronts what is. Marvel and surprise mix, dissolving preconceptions that clog the senses. The moment is an awakening of intelligence. Its natural expression is the smile.

According to legendary accounts, by the miraculous spirit of the laugh the Buddha conveyed his understanding. Sakyamuni was discussing his ideas when he arrived at a critical point. Finding no words, he lifted a single flower. All around him were blank looks except that of an old man, Mahakasyapa. The old man smiled, no more. His smile signified transmission of wonder. The Buddha perceived his awakening and pronounced Mahakasyapa his true successor.

The smile—is it not a return to an unlearned wonderment? An infant's smile spreads across her face with the bliss of existence. "The smile that flickers on baby's lips when he sleeps—does anybody know where it was born?" (Tagore). In the infancy of consciousness, in deep, dreamless sleep, the eternal mother reigns. The immutable realm is hers. Clothes and all ephemeral things with which the baby is dressed belong to the father. Sleeping, an infant becomes naked again. It rests beside the mother's breast, where its repose lacks no thing. All is sufficient, all is plenty. It is nourished simply by being where it has come to, unsapped by dream, perception, or attainment. There is wonder at a perfection of support, nothing more. From awareness, like a pocket of oxygen trying to escape the depths, an infant's smile rises to its lips.

Perfection of human consciousness is not, however, to be sought in a regression to infancy. Mahakasyapa's smile is a smile of nakedness, but a nakedness in the three realms—dream, dreamless sleep, and waking perception. An infant's smile is in his world, together with dreamer's and ego's. An infant's smile, its silent diffusion of laughter, is a gift wrought by the matrix of life. Life when whole manifests with a smile. Mahakasyapa's is an earning, a fruit of personal effort and self-initiated labors. It is an outcome—if *outcome* is the right word—of a commitment, tested by ordeal, and ripened by practice. It is, perhaps, an astonishment that the prize sought is already possessed and that, therefore, there is nothing, there has been nothing, and there will never be anything, to seek. The wholeness from which Mahakasyapa's smile floats upward stands both before and within him. His vision concludes he is not separate from the world that smiles, with the Buddha, at him. His smile is, therefore, not his, but an upturned lip of reality, welcoming the momentary guest of existence.

A thinker may ask, "What is the survival value of the laugh?" A pragmatic approach, typical of a metropolis, looks for an argument with laughter, one that imbues it with a power of adaptability for *Homo sapiens*. One could speak of how the laugh unflexes us and leaves us more flexible. We may benefit from its repeated pointing to our rigidity, fixed attitudes, and unbending precepts. It also awakens perception and refreshes a fatigued outlook. Suffering and weight of age are thereby reduced. The laugh is tonic to a good life.

What a ludicrous way of speaking! As if the laugh were one function in a bevy of functions that made up life. Such logic is frivolous insofar as it stops short of asking what life is for—asking, that is, the question of the laugh. No doubt a laugher lives longer and is prone to fewer diseases (unless ticklishness is one). But the avatar of ease itself, the laugh, releases one from life to Life. True, the one who laughs is able to accomplish many great things, but the high-spirited guardian comes with a different aim. Ease, harmony of the moment, is a posture of relation to one's situation. Absent from ease is restless expectation, a mind wagging the rest of the person. Being related, ease is able to respond to Need (Love's mother) without tension or retention. Ease always faces this relation, forever background to all human endeavor.

Ease, therefore, looks in a reverse direction. We whose concern is to leave a mark upon the world confront the outer with expressive energy. Ease is mind of the other, inward current. Together, ease and action complete a circulation. The breath also has a similar cycle, an incoming, energizing phase and an outgoing, enervating phase. The cycle is delicate and subject to disharmonizing forces from body, mind, and feelings. When imbalanced from, say, shallow, fearful breathing, circulation is incomplete, leading to rapid exhaustion of energies. The same is true of the deeper cycle of action and ease, ease and action. Yet our habit is to hold our breath just before an onset of acting. Not to breathe ease in or to hyperventilate action out produces a cataclysmic fatigue. One quickly ceases to be master of an undertaking and instead is "done to." Aim is lost, and act becomes simply an outcome of influences, not of our design or intention, impinging on the agent.

Reasons of health and exigence dictate the way of balance. "The world is ruled by letting things take their course" says the same thing; "it cannot be ruled by interfering" (Lao Tzu). To cease holding the breath is to allow circulation to reestablish itself. Similarly, to cease spending oneself in action is to let ease renew a sense of self. Both are nurturing of being. Yet tension, once habitual, becomes invisible. Breath held, act conspired after—the grasp must be forcibly broken. Just here enters the spirit of laughter. Try to hold on now! Fingers tickle in the grasp, muscles melt, and the breath, natural and unstrained, once again fills the lungs. Aahh. Good.

24

LADDERS

The trail abruptly ends in front of a sheer wall of rock. It had wound easily through scrub pine, following an escarpment from cleft to cleft. We had walked in each other's footsteps, a silent study of the mountain. Now we stare point blank ahead at gray slate that reaches up nearly to the sky's zenith. No handholds, too soft for protection, no way around. Spirits sink. How could we go on? Must we go back? Just then, from within a hidden chimney, comes the guide's cry, "A ladder!"

The magic power of ladders lies in their swift resolution of impasses. An unknown blocks the path, while on either edge yawns a precipitous drop. To retreat, or to forge ahead: The traditional horns of a dilemma. The solution appears upon lifting our eyes up. The ladder that begins with feet on the ground points to heaven. Thus Abraham stopped in midcareer in sacrificing his son Isaac and looked up. High in a cedar tree was a ram, provided for the burnt offering. Like a boy, Abraham used the tree's branches as a ladder. Climbing, he became one with all his ages and lived beyond them. The ladder brought a gift of heaven down to earth.

Ladders come to us themselves with ancient conundrums. The first involves a matter of time. Is the way between heaven and earth—wherein the everyday spirits ply—crossed in a single leap? Or are there steps that one after the other lead to the far side? Is knowledge gained suddenly or by a gradual raising of a veil? Rung by rung, ladders provide access to heights otherwise unbridgeable. They reveal that persistent effort lifts a climber skyward. They prove the value of an incremental approach to elevation.

There is a second conundrum. It involves a matter of direction. Do ladders go up or down? On earth, gravity is the predominant force. Terrestrial life is subject to its downward pull, its desire to level things, and its denial of differences in scale. Because of gravity, water seeks the lowest horizon, boulders plummet from a mountaintop, and sand and dust are attracted to the depths. The pull of gravity to the center has an effect of flattening one thing on top of another. Only that which resists gravity survives. The cost to daily life is compression of time and distortion of care. Time foreshortens, and charm lapses from what we care for. Gravity dispirits us. It makes for drabness, dullness, and murkiness, and leaves a posture stooped. It is amnesia of height.

When not informed by this subtle spirit, we are lost to ourselves. We are then prone to an organic forgetfulness of the upright position—that position wherein vertebrae make a ladder from tailbone to base of skull. A human body is a sack of flesh slung around a ladder, with structural supports and a locomotive option added on. That we, the ladder, are made to stand upright irreversibly distinguishes us from the rest of the animal kingdom. No longer do we see with eyes on the same horizontal as the spine, but from a horizontal on the top—a perpendicular. Like vision, a passage of energies also is transformed by tilting the skeletal ladder upright. With the uppermost rung nearer to celestial influences, human alignment acquires startling new possibilities. With aid of this spirit, man, woman, or child can resonate with the nearness of an inner divinity.

To return to the conundrum: Ladders protect against an amnesia of height. Ladders have the ability to neutralize ill effects of gravity. They work by uplifting a body—a sympathetic work since the body while on a ladder lifts itself. Movement—up or down—is counter to a leveling tendency whose issue is loss of discretion. Aloft, muscles decompress, while a suffocating weight of care is channeled into the problem of balance. Fear of heights gives more proof of the point: One grows afraid only when one drops one's focus on organic equilibrium. All ladders are pointed heavenward. For anyone on a ladder, the riddle is no riddle. All ladders travel up.

There is a third conundrum. It involves a matter of origin. Where do ladders come from? Do they begin on earth, reaching up, or in heaven, dropping down? The question is one of some subtlety. Though ladders are raised against gravity, an impulse to regain height descends from above. At the very same moment as careworn tension melts, an ascending vision appears. Memory of the skyward direction is preserved in heaven, safe from the distractions of earthbound existence. Ladders originate in the immortal realm so that we—forgetfulness withal—may be able to reach that which waits undying within us.

The riddle tells that, for humans, ladders are for climbing. Even going down a ladder is a climb that needs no less muscular exertion than going up. We must always climb, because the ladder's origin lies on a level higher than our own, born of the earth's gravity, and all ladders sustain that origin. Only a being not subject to the laws of earth can truly *descend*. A duality of direction is summarized in Jacob's dream in which a ladder extends from heaven to earth. Men, whole nations, climb while angels spring down "from one step to the next, giving a little lift of the wings" (Levertov, "The Jacob's Ladder"). The way up is arduous, the way down, easy. Knowledge of reality descends to us in a moment of harmony. A choiceless freedom permeates the depths. By contrast, determination marks the upward direction. It is a striving—to spark a memory of balance—that lights an ascent.

The genius of ladders lies in design. They push off from earth with their feet and gain height only through repeated lateral support. Sidepieces must be related through crosspieces, or else the ladder remains a pole. Ladders thus rely on a secret principle—that the vertical can be attained only by strict attention to the horizontal. The same principle operates in the cross, which is a ladder with a missing sidepiece. The principle is rarely understood. The ladder (or cross) provides a way of ascent through care for that which cannot ascend, which always remains on the same level. Height becomes a matter of greater inclusiveness rather than sheer verticality. Fear (or its inverse, rapture) of heights forgets the indirectness of a climb. It moves ahead of itself, obsessed by a notion of utter perpendicularity. The pathology dreams of an angelic existence. It rejects a human way with ladders, striving to retain balance on each rung.

Ladders, I said, retain a memory of upward movement. On the ground, gravity compresses perception so as to eliminate scale. There is the one and only horizontal. Climbing above, one leaves behind flatness while recovering height. A vision of a graduated order of things—scale—grows clearer with each upward step. Here, an optical illusion born of heights comes into play. The nearer the sky, the larger it looms and the farther off it grows. High up, the ground, by contrast, is smaller and nearer. We are smaller yet. Relative size is born of a vision of elevation. There is a corollary fact. Relation—letting the parts be a whole—shows itself only through scale. Different parts relate to one another only under the influence of a higher unity—thus do ladders begin in heaven. With the greater vastness above, the lesser below, we find ourselves at a midway point, on a ladder that joins sky and ground. The soaring spirit of ladders supports our perilous station.

In the scale of things, how high up can we go? Are there limits to a human ascent? Remember how it is, climbing. The ladder gives an ever-shifting view of sky and ground. Change from one rung to the next is more apparent the more effortful a step. Still, there is the moment (known to every child) of discovering a new place suspended in air. Here one meets the spirit face-to-face. The discovery marks a transformation—an influx of an openness to replace the former closure. Ladders are sites of transformation. Mounting, the one who stands above is different from the one who stood below. With each step, limitation changes meaning. With each step, the "I can" reaches higher.

Care on ladders is directed to the rungs. When we embrace a horizontal, each rung has its specific demand, and danger. On lower rungs, care is primarily for one's own sake. Higher up, other things are urgently felt: the need for love, service, prayer, the way, and the teaching itself. Only presence is a constant. When it is lost and balance is taken for granted, gravity happily claims its next victim. When lack of care is the cause, to fall is to lose the gains garnered by lift. It is to lose mastery and freedom, since knowledge of place and order sets one free. Whether one falls with awareness or not greatly affects outcome. If one falls off the ladder, with hammer, saw, boards, and crowbar, one might save one's life through one's awareness. Attention in midflight disposes of potential hazards and prepares one's body for contact. To crash is to fall without preparation.

Almost single-handedly, the spirit of ladders gives earthbound bodies proof of height. Visible ladders rise through a third dimension, perpendicular to gravity's flatland. Ladders invisible to ordinary eyes also are known. Their existence is understood analogically, through our movement against heaviness of all kinds. They ascend through higher dimensions, enabling inner experiences of elevation. While they are still ladders, their design differs from those of everyday life. Their rungs are not set at uniform intervals. At times, the step up is shorter, at other times longer. The fact of orderly variation is part of the law of scale. One must assimilate it in order to pass upward.

Ascent to height is, as in music, up a scale. The musical scale shows a regular incremental advance as pitch rises. But one note follows another by differences not always uniform. In two places, the ascent slows to a half step before picking up the usual pace. To increase the pitch at the same rate as before produces a misstep. Scales are ladders, and ladders into the invisible, scales. A wrong step is followed by the sound of a crash.

Ladders greet our dailiness on all sides. Who hasn't climbed a ladder today? The stone porch steps, spiral stairs to a loft, a chain fire escape, a folding ladder, the library ladder on rails, an aluminum utility ladder, a rope ladder to the tree house, the apple picker's ladder with pinched-in sides. There are specialty ladders: hook-and-ladder fire ladders, ropework ladders to the foresail, lifesaving ladders from helicopters. Then there is much that imitates ladders: snail shells, leaves spirling up a stalk, whorls on a caterpillar, thumbprints on a hand. A spiral is just a circle inspired by the ladder.

The ubiquity of ladders reveals another startling fact about this munificent spirit. A bridge is a reclining ladder. A bridge supports human weight against the implacable urge of gravity. It allows one to make a crossing and to end up farther along the way than before. Like anything else on a recline, a bridge breeds indolence. Horizontal, bridges bring a forgetfulness. To move from one side to the other costs nothing. A keen edge of awareness—always to be paid for—is lost. Unaware, we cross over to the other side barely acknowledging the moment of suspension in the middle.

This is because we walk on a skin of things. To redesign a bridge helps uncover the way inward. Remove railing, tear away superstructure, leave bare girders—or better yet, a simple rope suspension—and a kinship with ladders is immediately felt. A bridge is no longer inert matter but vibrates with hazards of transition. Of all qualities of crossing, urgency is the most important. Urgency is the tempo of the intermediate zone. Urgency is also most useful to us, since urgency loves the highest pitch of activity. With urgency, a climb does not languish from lack of initiative. We are guided by a depth of caring whose origin lies beyond the top of the ladder.

Yet the ladder too becomes merely a means. If all ladders were portable and had to be set in place each time, it would be different. Then we would be returned to the heft of working the internal ladder— our spinal column—that balances brain against brawn. Often enough, the magical operation of this spirit is felt only in a result. One climbs to the top of steep stairs (a fixed ladder), to the attic, and breathes a memory quite different from the fragrances of nostalgia. A storeroom at the top, the attic gathers and keeps things free from perishing in a taken-for-granted realm below. Furnishings of infancy, childhood toys, bibelots of youth, coins of several passages—time surrounds each with a stillness. To witness a jumble of epochs is to stand clear of a past, which is what the ladder invites. An impress of elevation, however, is often faint, as if raised by hairbreadths rather than yards. Do we honor the small as well as the great? The ladder brings a new perspective that, had we ourselves carried the ladder, would welcome and accept.

Most ladders we find already in place, humanmade and heaven-laid. Occasionally, however, genius discovers an unknown ladder, so that we may stand on our fathers' shoulders and see anew. These explorers, both recorded and unrecorded, leave behind a question. What does compassion do with the ladder after ascent? By a moun-taineer's logic, ladders once gone up have no use. All means are rela-tive and absolutely to be abolished when a climb is done, "for there is one," Pound writes

Whose smile more availeth
Then all the age-old knowledge of thy books.

(*"The Eyes"*)

To leave no trace, one "must so to speak throw away the ladder after he has climbed up it" (Wittgenstein, *Tractatus* 6.54). From a stand-point of rigor, compassion dictates strangely. It is not a matter of mak-ing things easy, but of allowing the other to find a way to ease. In its career, value lies in an obstacle, a hard ascent, a riddled path. To find a ladder where otherwise is only impasse thus deflates the value—the search. It presumes us to be gods who seek no thing, a presumption most heavy to bear.

But ladders embrace a duality, as do we who occupy the rungs. As everyday spirits, ladders contact both the relative and the absolute and allow commerce between the two. Compassion, even when sagely, is not always absolute. An unknown mountaineer who spends a week carving a ladder from scrub pine leaves behind a legacy. Others' climbs are possible because of this work. Some achieve a height not otherwise open to them. To the one who devised the ladder, a great debt of grat-itude is owed. He or she risked compassion that might have interfered with personal attainment. The risk always is to interfere in the name of helping. The risk is also to withhold in the name of rigor. Between the two sides, a sage walks the edge—which is the ladder so narrowed as to become rungless.

25

WILD GEESE

They lunge across a dawn sky. They disturb the stillness of earth sleeping below with their high, almost inaudible cries. Spring has not yet come to flower, is no more than a promise of warmth at noonday. Yet they come at dawn, before gray frosted night has faded, insistently drawing our gaze upward—and we to our upward gaze—to peer, to search, to watch the sky. It is April, and wild geese are flying north.

Throughout the day, wedge after wedge passes with whispering aloofness. In low cloud, mist, or dark, there is no more than that sound, unless an ear can pick up the whirring of wings. Only brightness of day lets them barely stand out, a wedge driving through an impassive sky. And calls continuing, backward and forward, side to side, as if flight were made blasting a way through the air. Afterward, silence is heavy with them.

Thus wild geese pass. Rarely does vision call us to their presence. Instead, it is a faint hiss of the almost inaudible. In flight, wild geese soar just this side of the other, eternal, unspeakable, unchanging world. They are a last sigh owed gravity before passing wholly over.

Or a first sigh on passing back. For like all everyday spirits, their motion ceaselessly reverses itself, finishing one phase before contradicting itself, intent on the cycle. The unfathomable urge of the cycle is to return to its starting point. Wild geese, earliest harbingers of spring, reappear in mid-October, heading south at first frost. Their sound is no less, no more, than what it usually is, but more urgent.

169

Northward, they embrace green shoots of life. Southward, they flee brittle husks of dormancy, sleep, and living death.

Back and forth over intermediate miles, the geese wander, driven. What drives them drives all everyday spirits, "the envoys and interpreters that ply between heaven and earth" (Plato). It is need for food. To nourish vital and inner aspects of their being, they draw energies from the two worlds. As a by-product, they blend, mingle, and cross-pollinate what otherwise remains separate. They perform their function at an enormous pitch of activity. So it seems to us when we humans are virtually motionless, grave, lacking in initiative, and stagnant. When in momentary relation with some spirit, our perspective undergoes an abrupt, inexplicable shift. We also enjoy an intensity similar to theirs. Taken up by their whirling dance, we become partners, brokers, allies,...and lovers. We too are spirited by forces from which they draw reality.

If we are the geese's lovers (even for a moment), we abandon our obstructed condition to seek the same food as they—commingling the higher with the lower. For when we join with them, differences in refinement and level are annulled. During that ephemeral union, we put on their knowledge and power "before the indifferent beak" lets us drop (Yeats). Related by a moment of love, we fly with our breath toward what is always present to our presence. We inhabit our beloved's space and for that time make it our own. So it is with wild geese, whose primal urge to migrate joins us to them in their flight.

For what food do the geese migrate? Succulent stalks of young arrowroot in the lake's shallows are a magnet. But the animal body has not been starved in the southern feeding grounds. Famine has not driven them to journey again, but a stronger force. Change is the food they seek. In change, new replaces worn, untasted, and charmless—and the just-born, the dying. For change, they race the sun as it climbs north, refusing rest and replenishment for days. For change, they navigate by changeless stars and utter hoarse cries that rend the changeless realm in twain. Secret knowledge stirs their accomplishment in its simplicity: In change is the only constancy.

The flight of geese is restless. Birds rove for new positions, taking turns at being leader. The formation bends, skews, breaks, and regroups according to the moment. The group strives to embody a form constantly rippled by wind and rendered imperfect. It is as if an artist's hand—the quivering of its flesh—is unable to bring her intention to the paper. A wedge shape is the shape of a flying goose, and the formation tries to bring the goose self, moment after moment, into being. Its only success is approximation—unless in darkest night it abolishes all hazard and secretly incarnates the goose in flight. That is unlikely, since the cries never trail away to silence, but persist in a kind of homing signal. It is a signal one emits, giving one's whereabouts while still journeying, still looking for home.

Wild geese in flight seek change within the cycle—spring feeding grounds, nesting, breeding, perpetuating—and, at the same time, constancy—the form of Goose itself. They march in a parade of seasons while simultaneously announcing that which is of all seasons. A solitary gander makes reference to the same form as a wedge does almost inaudibly above storm clouds. Flying, the goose perpetually points toward what it is not yet but strives to embody. The peculiar power of the everyday spirit derives from the goose's unceasing traversal of the space between seeming and being. It is not what it appears to be and seems not to be what it is. It lives in a zone where appearance and reality clash and waver before the eyes like two opposing colors. Its habitat is the intermediate. To and fro, near and far, it quests endlessly for the Self.

That the form wild geese fly toward is the Self—having no set form—explains the spirit's peculiar power. Because their flight pattern tends without success toward a goose's shape, their failure brings an annunciation. In the midst of gray April drizzle, we are called from preoccupations to an invisible passage aloft. The call comes from an inner skin of audibility, a very fine sandpaper over the nerves. Because their cry articulates an unfilled lack between approximation and realization, it conveys recognition. Then, a secret chamber opens in the back of a mind to reveal the presence of that which reconciles seeming and being. We stand in the vertical, through which migrates—top to bottom—an energy to unify the whole. This also is the flight of wild geese, whose sound brings unexcelled attainment.

Flight's muscular exertion is toward the commonplace, repose in dwelling and procreating. The flight of wild geese is thus an interval, an intention, that aims at that which it is not. Other flights—from fear or lying—are without end and, therefore, are condemned to be forever mindless of what they are. They enact perpetual betrayal or refusal of form. The passage of wild geese, however, is that of awareness. The duality of wild geese is like that of the breath, in and out, not plus and minus. The flight stops for a change and, when change is timeworn, reverses itself and moves on.

Some everyday spirits have a double. In blending immiscible energies of the two shores by force of its genius, an everyday spirit may give birth to a parody (or concealment) of itself—a, so to speak, foolish younger sibling. This gives rise in the workaday world to a confusion of identity. The duality of the wild geese expresses itself in the distance between air and ground, flying and waddling. An earthbound goose is ungainly, ill tempered, greedy, and raucous. Scavenger, aggressor, braggart, lecher, it evokes nothing of height. Its voice is a strident hiss forced as from a throat constricted by anger. When alarmed, it rises to a level of cacophony. The citizens of Athens valued its flock of geese in the lowly capacity of watchdog. No one could approach the city without inciting the geese to riot. Athenians unwittingly sacrificed the double of this hysterical, foolish goose, the goose sublime in flight. For purposes of utility, wings were clipped, thereby robbing people of a softer, more penetrating call to Self. Athens, safe from enemy attack, slept more easily—ears plugged to the shock wave of autumn migration. No remorse betrayed her habits of tyranny and self-indulgence to herself.

In the fairy tale, the gander is a mean, threatening intruder, a greedy thief. A young girl offers him a poppyseed cake. After accepting, he takes another and another, and finally explodes from overeating. His feathers are put to good use in pillows and dusters. Here, the gander as double caricatures a wild goose's appetite for change. He endlessly wants more of the same mutable substance, until he bursts from it. To eat leaves him more leaden, more earthbound, less expressive of this other, lighter nature. Only a detonation from inside sends him scattering heavenward, toward wild geese in flight.

By contrast, a sacred gander of the Vedas feeds on *amrita*, stuff of immortality. Even as he walks the earth, he is already in flight, as if each step were a descent from celestial wandering. His name barely snatches him from formlessness, or at least its very utterance bears witness to the other world. In Sanskrit he is known as *hamsa*. To pronounce the word is to evoke the *arche*-sound that stretches between time and eternity, *Om*.

> Now it has elsewhere been said: 'This, namely *a*, *u*, and *m*
> (= *Om*), is the sound-form of the Self.'
>
> (*Maitri Upanisad* 6.5)

The first syllable of his name, *ham*-, echoes the ever-present sound *Om*. Deep sleep of infancy, the dream, and the everyday realm—the three states of human consciousness—are thereby traversed. Speaking of the gander, one passes from unequaled repose wherein laughter and lullaby are born, through seductions of dream life, to the overconcerned pitch of ordinary existence. Having surveyed all things human, one passes beyond to energies of the upper world. The immortal realm, the fourth state (*turiyo*), includes the other three as an acorn contains an oak, or a germ cell a whole family's lineage. Borne by the *hansa*-sound, one crosses an inner space in graduated leaps until one comes to a background resonance. All is dissolved in a sound no different from a sound of oneself.

From deep need, one utters the gander's name. The place from where *hansa* resounds is not known in advance. A name roves just as a gander wanders. An ear must be attuned to surprises. Straining over waterlogged leaves of last fall or late-winter muck, one is suddenly recalled to the loft of heaven by a shrill cry. A timeworn mind is sloughed off, and another mind, sleek and sharp, glistens like the gander's cloak in dawn light. This mind reaches backward, both to the past and to beyond the past, to the ever-present. Bent back, one is also returned to childhood. There the gander lives, too, to open the storybook for a child, and the child's heart to a love of things of heaven and earth.

Did not old Mother Goose

> when she wanted to wander
> ride on the back of a very fine gander?

Nursery rhyme, sibling of the lullaby, echoes with sound and rhythm evoked by the gander's name. *Hamsa*, homeless one, wanderer, itinerate Self. To let attention wander over things of the dwelling place is to honor the suchness of each one. To take in each in its time is to love what life brings. To respect the form of everything is to be at ease in activity. The gander lays provision for these accomplishments.

> Goosey, goosey gander, where dost thou wander?
> Upstairs and downstairs and in my lady's chamber.

A joyful vision roves playroom, kitchen, and outdoors and is undisguised as to its source. Manifesting without concealment, it meanders over this and that, illuminating objects. Its field forever changing, a gander's roving eye is constant only in its appetite to take things in, transform their inert form to vivid experience, and uplift the world. A child who spends hours adrift in its flight thus knows both the constancy and the fickleness of love. A migratory rhythm that visits dream, dreamless sleep, and the waking state carries a child aloft to take a survey of the world and give back the measure of human life.

To migrate is to set off wandering toward a particular place. Wild geese's procession across the sky is full of purpose but also winding turns, exchanges of position, rest stops, and improbable detours. An intelligence that instinctively seeks change guides their flight. So too with a child who shares the way with a wanderer. When does the goose's flight turn fanciful? When the creature flies north to the snows, or south to the summer, purpose is out of kilter with reality. Correspondence with the seasons confers reason on an undertaking. That which has its time and place has its will. For a child, to be carried away from concerns that press in upon a heart is the gander's blessing. When childhood fades and the gander's call does not, the danger of this everyday spirit becomes apparent. The wild-goose chase—pursuit of the ungettable—arises when aim has been dragged aside by impulse. A rush of wings in the air, wild honking, an indefatigable striving: These energies serve the single purpose for which wild geese live—to return themselves to their origin. Scotch the purpose, and flight turns self-destructive.

In infancy, awareness drives no wedge between the potential and the actual in being. Ever-present and undivided, it meets a presence of things on the inside. A quiet moment will return us to an unruptured present whose breath relates to the source of breathing. In between, life calls us outside. Playfriends, the woods, Jack Frost, arithmetic: Attention is drawn toward the everyday. A child suffers withdrawal in mood, illness, or precocious gravity—without means of expression. Only its aftereffects are felt—loss of easy communion with the wandering gander—and then but faintly. Actuality comes to be what is, potentiality, what might be dreamed. Life delineates the two inasmuch as, when a child is with herself, potentiality is restored to her. Otherwise, act and deed command all her energies. What begins as a slow waddle, matching steps with life, ends as a frenzied march. Achievement is actuality, potentiality is nothing.

We are heirs to a child's loss. Because change has come in its season, we are powerless to reverse our fortunes. Life lives itself through us, and, by and large, events perpetrate themselves on us, who lack an awareness of choice. A wedge has been driven. Potentiality lives isolated in a separate chamber from actuality. A king's son cannot find his kingdom, a true daughter is abused by her stepmother. Then without warning, from high up, the wedge splits the sky. Wild geese are flying! Seasons are changing and from the heart of change, the constancy of the wandering gander. His call abides as it once did in the nursery. The tear in being is healed in this moment, and each moment in which we, listening, remember a true force of his name.

26

THE FRONTIER GUARD

The frontier guard has the gaze of one who looks both ways. Facing the desert beyond, he stands with eyes in the back of his head. Turned toward the heartlands, he is mindful of events in the outer world. His station is small, an outpost with scant furnishings. His command is a few feet in either direction, the edge of a territory. Because he surveys leave-takings and entries, his authority extends thousands of miles beyond the squat hut of his dwelling. "Desolate castle, the sky, the wide desert" (Pound, "Lament of the Frontier Guard"). What passes the gate, out or in, passes only with his agreement. Hence, integrity of two vastnesses—inside and out—lies within his power. The gaze of the frontier guard neither wavers nor sleeps. It commends itself at all times to visitors.

Solitude is the guardsman's cloak. He wraps it around himself as a uniform, an identity, and a protection. It is not an amulet for magic or a cloth with mystical powers, for it is made of human vulnerability and has a strength only of that substance. Solitude brings the guard to look at himself both ways, from outside in and from inside out. Fear, loneliness, and longing occupy a foreground whose distant background is composed and vibrant. Solitude is the last frontier, whose chain of command ends leagues away in a populous center, the metropolis. Solitude is a margin between the two realms, a skin that holds them apart, and a membrane that allows the two to interpenetrate.

Solitude keeps the frontier guard wary. Since it knows itself, it brooks no intrusion. Not by stealth or deception can anyone cross the border, since solitude is an absolute barrier. One either has solitude or has none. Any subtraction is annihilation. Hence, to enter the guard's solitude is to annul it, an event easy to recognize. In wariness, solitude reveals a kinship with wholeness. Both are absolutely intolerant of any partition and absolutely distinct from any fraction. Both possess a secret of relationship, because each is related to itself. The words disclose a family resemblance. Solitude derives from the Latin *solus* (now a stage direction), which is ultimately akin to the Greek *holos*, whole. Thus, integrity—the guardsman's keep—shapes a fabric of solitude and keeps a mind ever watchful against encroachment and compromise.

The thin strip—the frontier itself—is not established by divine decree. It is a contour of artifice, happenstance, and vague influence that validates one territorial claim against another. Wherever it travels, west or east, through valleys or mountains, it leaves an indelible mark upon the land. It has great meaning. It sets up a zone, a region, an empire, a kingdom, a nation. The frontier is imbued with awareness—personified by its guard—the way the skin is. It senses what is foreign. It is able to because, in the great vastness of nature, it itself is foreign, unnatural, alien. Belonging to neither world, it stands between them, barrier to both.

Whether arbitrarily or not, the frontier, like a skin, divides off a space from the rest. The act is obverse to the guardsman's solitude that makes space whole. Both are important to the complexion of this everyday spirit. To segregate a smaller region establishes a need for its own internal order. An intelligence thus arises in the lesser space. Its ability to communicate with the greater intelligence is a new attainment, never before known with undivided space.

Separation into zones is a way of increase. "The many become one, and are increased by one" (Whitehead). What exponentially increases is a power to communicate. Prior to the frontier, solitude—oneself being with oneself—is the mode. Subsequently, one relates with the other. Unimaginable richness is born of otherness. As with many everyday spirits, contradiction vitalizes the frontier guard. His aspects combine incommensurables. Wherever we look, opposition flaunts itself. The frontier is a membrane that joins the two sides. It is that which must be penetrated in order to consummate an act of communication. As an impediment, the frontier's fulfillment lies in being breached.

A human body exemplifies the metaphor of the frontier guard. Within the skin—the outermost limit—energies either seek embrace with one another or rove in chaotic abandon. Anarchy or order is determined by the frontier's sensitivity. When skin shows discretion—keeping intrusive influences out, letting beneficent ones in—the whole body falls under laws of harmony. Easy interchange occurs with the environment, and health prospers. When "the creature-world beholds the open" (Rilke), pores are its eyes. If they let in too much or too little, an organism becomes imbalanced, overstimulated, or underfed. A body teaches that permeability is life, and its privation, a death.

The fact is a lesson in paradox. From the center emanates all authority. But if the skin authorizes passage of things in and out—and determines the state of the whole—the center is on the outside. Imagine a bowl somehow pulled inside out. A human body is such an inverted vessel. Its contents are perpetually inpouring, and what it seems to contain is in reality external to it. With sensitivity on its periphery, it wears its heart on its sleeve. A heart is an emblem of the frontier guard.

Like a body, margins of a region are invested with an awareness. The work of the guardsman partakes of it. He watches the passing-over without himself ever leaving. He monitors identities of those entering and departing. Passports, customs documents, and bills of lading assist him. He is on the lookout for those who are despised, deplored, and condemned as well as those awaited, applauded, and eagerly sought. His judgment carries finality. He is the one of first and last resort. Without his scrutiny, a person can vanish without a trace.

It almost happens that way with Lao Tzu. By tradition, "the sage wears rough clothing and holds the jewel in his heart" (Lao Tzu). Who is able to recognize him? Only one who, guarding the order of the body politic, is aware of the reversal of skin and core, perimeter and center. Only one who knows a human vessel is somehow pulled inside out. Only one who breathes a concealment of the frontier in the rude hut and simple life of its guardsman. The guard, on meeting Lao Tzu, is met with the frontier. Lao Tzu is the frontier of humanity. He reaches the farthest and journeys to the limit. He fills a truth of being human to the highest degree.

Lao Tzu lives in the homeless district, the no-man's-land that stretches between the mortal and the immortal. His life lies on a margin that divides one from the other. It is marginal in belonging not to him but to a power he makes himself available to. He is marginal man. Since "the divine will not mingle directly with the human," communication depends on transitional beings such as him (Plato). Contact with each realm through a third, "the medium," allows for mutual enrichment without violating the law of separation. Because he is in transition and neither mortal nor immortal, Lao Tzu can address both realms. Human and angel both listen to his words.

Beings charged with indirect communication take their form according to a strict logic. They—the everyday spirits—seem to be ordinary objects while representing a channel through which the higher relates to our level. Ladders, bridges, ropes, and bowls are commonplace means of connecting above with below through ingenious technologies. I could add other devices—funnels, incense, pennants, the well—but do not. In each case, the joining force, the spirit, conveys energy from one to the other through unknown routes. Lao Tzu personifies the frontier. At a line dividing the ordinary from the extraordinary, we invariably meet the work of Lao Tzu.

The frontier guard's office is to discern who belongs to the land. The well-being of everyone rests with his power to let only those pass who so merit. Confronting Lao Tzu, the guard confronts someone who belongs to no land. He appears to be of little use, with no wealth or power. If he sends the old man off, what loss? If he refuses to grant an exit visa, what gain? What is to be done? As he ponders, the other is already hauling himself up along the jagged rocks beyond the pale. With what unexpected ease does the old man move! Watching, the frontier guard experiences a peculiar shedding of scales from his eyes. He sees how each thing has its opposite and how neither really fits, as if every quality were foreign to the man. Nothing sticks, because there is nothing to grasp onto. Lao Tzu's practice is a cultivation of foreignness. He stands outside of himself.

Wherever he goes, the old man remains apart from demands of place and time. Anger, grief, pity, greed, despair, and fear pass through him without gaining a foothold. They provoke no reaction, hence nothing holds them back. Human beings feel many things as a matter of course as part of life. Lao Tzu does not. But because he is foreign to his own nature, and it to him, Lao Tzu understands nature. "Returning to the source is stillness, which is the way of nature" (Lao Tzu). Because it is natural to desire, to need, and to expect, he does not refuse the impulse. But because he stands apart from his nature, he is able to respond to a higher Nature. Like the frontier guard, he remains inside, watching out, and at the same time outside, watching in. In this consists his foreignness.

The door also is a frontier. It opens and closes. It thereby controls access to a space, inside or out, via a passageway through which a guest may enter or exit. A doorkeeper is an urban counterpart to the frontier guard. She watches both directions, coming and going, with an eye to the entire assemblage—building, hall, or room under her keep. Her practice is discretion. A glance, a casual remark, an offhand question, is enough to provoke a telling response and reveal her mastery of the situation. Who should be barred from entry, who should be contacted before leaving, who should be immediately sought: These are specific exercises of doorkeeping. They are enactments of an autonomy of the one at the door. That she defers to no one is evidence that the center of command lies there, next to the outside, at the frontier of the gathering. Mastery of the door seals the destiny of the interior, and incompetence its doom.

At his frontier station, the guard prepares his evening meal. Smoke rises to a cloudless sky. Water boils in a rice pot. From the outpost, barrens stretch in every direction. The nearest town is over the horizon. An elemental simplicity returns to the world. Each thing bears a living relation to the others. "Transparent beams of moonset flicker on the sand" (Tu Fu, "Midnight"). There is motion, but as in a still life. Composition dissolves to reveal simple substances that make it up. Mutual respect is the operant principle. Each simple takes its place free from encroachment upon, or intrusion within by, any other. Each wears its essential face, while the composite has an accidental quality. The sky could have been cloud-streaked, the wall, unbroken—but it is not so. The frontier is a restatement of the simple.

At the capital, in the emperor's palace, the pageant is endless. Feasts, debates, hunts, performances, and masked balls fill every available moment. Importunate chatter rules the air, while encounters depend entirely on accident and chance. Advisers of state march in after the magicians leave. From the milieu—that of a composite—an empire is ruled, provinces organized, taxes levied, honors accorded, and virtue sought. To the emperor, the frontier is a distant outpost of questionable value that tests the extent of his almost weakened will. Only when "the Emperor's drunken soldiery are abed" (Yeats) does a real relation of perimeter to center appear. The veils adorning the composite fall. The king bears the likeness of a frontier guard!

When night quiet returns the royal palace and guardsman's hut to their habits, it is a time to examine frontiers. Are they rightly set? Do they protect and conceal? Do they maintain order and allow a flourishing? The questions dictate "the process of looking straight into one's own heart and acting on the results" (Pound, *Confusius, The*

Great Digest). In moonlight, one stands on craggy outcroppings where wall meets desert and looks back toward the intricacies of the palace. The distance is great and filled with many diversions. Fear of immensity or love of entertainment saps initiative from the vigil. Often a look does not penetrate the complexities of the kingdom and falls shy. The center is not restored to simplicity. But when the spirit of the frontier enters the heart of a king, nothing human is impossible.

Looked into, a heart looks up. Thus a look goes both ways. A heart's downward influences lighten and grow transparent. Being seen by one so distant, a heart relinquishes its pet notion, of being the center of the universe. For it too serves as a frontier of a more distant and elevated center. To its frontier guard, it gives orders. But orders come to it from one of still greater authority. The heart is thus uplifted in obedience, for that is the practice of the frontier guard. Its look is of obedience, and what it orders done is that which is in accord with heaven.

27

WIND

A t the desert's edge, rock has been worked by an invisible force into pillars of time. On a mountain peak, granite takes the form of a face molded by an intangible power. Uncanny beauty, a windswept presence, stands as witness to a passage of the heaven-sent to the earthbound and back again. That which effects change remains beyond sight and touch. We are left to ponder signature and intent of its maker, wind.

Wind flies up and down, from valleys below sea level to the thinnest air, never still. The atmosphere is a medium devised to allow immiscible influences from heaven and earth to mingle and grow fond of one another. That which stirs, folds, and mixes these otherwise separate energies is wind. Wind is the middle world's purposive self-agitation through which earth is elevated and heaven renewed. It is a fertilizing agent, spreading spores and seeds of earth, but not only earth. Lore attests to divine insemination by wind. Boreas, the north wind, once raped Oreithyia, daughter of the king of Athens. Pliny records folk legend that has it that mares conceive by turning hindquarters to the wind.

In ceaseless motion, wind is the very image of an everyday spirit, soaring with wings (at root, the same word as wind) through ever-present air. Its demeanor shows the two faces of a spirit, one of alarm, surprise, uncanniness, and terror, the other of healing, affection, sweetness, and balm. Swirling or buffeting, cascading or fluttering, wind is, as Plato says, "neither moral nor immortal,

183

for in the space of a day he will be now, when all goes well with him, alive and blooming, and now dying, to be born again by virtue of his father's nature, while what he gains will always ebb away as fast. (*Symposium* 203e)

Constant in its inconstancy, wind touches our existence intermittently, to intensify a moment of life, whether of joy or sorrow.

On many days, wind bears tidings of chance. The wonders or disasters wrought by wind epitomize a force of purposeless causation—an oak tree torn down by a gale, revealing a treasure chest buried at its roots. Toss a handful of blossoms to the wind, and note the pattern they leave on the floor. See the direction of a weather vane in the morning, and set out for there. These are ways of divination, which means discernment of an indeterminate element amidst the already-known. Wind is an ideal oracle. What it brings is accidental, contingent, random, unaccountable, and fortuitous. Dice fall, a roulette wheel spins, and wind blows. The unforeseeable—great and small—thus enters human existence. To a householder, it is a power outage caused by a windstorm just before a dinner guest arrives. To a historian, it is the Spanish Armada's defeat against all odds at the hands of a freak nor'easter. Wind bursts upon the scene, rattling window shades and blowing where it listeth, it makes Tom O'Bedlam rave and Lear lose his wits. It leaves the world topsy-turvy, for by the time it dies down, a fool has gained the service of a king.

A vase toppled over by a breeze spills water on a freshly inked manuscript and leaves a peculiar blot. The chance event defies human choice. The will strives for a predictable outcome, well-formed syntax, and a pleasing phrase. It seizes control over the machinery of action and rules with an iron hand, lest a glitch or ungrammaticality arise. It instruments a frame of concepts to support its writing exercise. Repeated use makes their causal bias as familiar as the tension that holds a pen. Will also restricts attention to avoid the counteroptions of going for a walk or listening to music. Enter the wind. "The wind that driveth the wits away" (*King Lear*). An upset vase may be an occasion of panic or black rage. Or it may be a breath of fresh air, if the value of chance is felt. A ruined manuscript is exchanged for a glimpse into another order, free from self-will. A meaningless blotch becomes a mark of unknown import, a cipher or a code. Wind blows open the door. Who comes in?

Thus the riddle of chance bothers choice. The moment arrests our incessant calculations: What to do, how to do it, will doing it bring profit, whom to ask for help? Cessation shifts value back to what now takes place, apart from a will's projects. The curtain wafts in a light breeze, and a fragrance of jonquils beckons us to partake. The stop is unplanned, but who would refuse? Unable to answer, we put choice aside. A choiceless freedom stirs. A window through which wind blows opens to an extraordinary event. We are returned to the Life within life.

Because we are eager to win, choice is a hard thing. Adversity nurtures our ability to make choices, and retribution builds our character. Choice worries the brow, creasing it over time. This is because choice needs to prove itself muscularly. No resistance, no choice. It rears itself in opposition to things and levers a body against the world. Determination and persistence temper it more. How strong is it, really? "The softest thing in the universe" breaks up the hardest thing, Lao Tzu writes. Choice does not readily yield, melt, unflex, relax, or flow, but holds to its decision. Strangely, it resists alternatives. It endures its own refusal not to follow them. Impervious, impenetrable, it sets itself apart from a wider view, minding only its uniqueness. It camouflages its brittleness and fear of ambiguity within a tower of accomplishment.

To stop a choice-hardened mind, the wind needs only to show a little devil or threaten severity. Mind takes notice. If not a pine-scented northerly, there is always a drastic measure—the tornado. Usually but a chance wind restores the moment. Chance is a windflower, the anemone, that clings to its love, the moment. For chance brings change, and with wind comes change. Change is perceived organically, through a body's windows. Wind lifts branches, rearranging a garden's lighting. Wind rustles the pines, sounding a note from distant childhood. Wind carries the brackish smell of a salt marsh or spice from a thick fern cover, remaking the appetites. Wind slaps the skin coldly, waking pores. What can fail to respond but an oblivion? Even an insensate boulder has an awareness etched in time by the wind.

Wind blows through a body's windows, singing. The wind's special quality makes it impossible to ignore. Roving air currents parallel a current of time in which one swims. That flux alone has constancy but is itself the river of change. The wind sings of impermanence, and who demurs?

Wind awakens an organic awareness by tingling hairs on the arm, roaring in the ears, or icing the toes. As a body remembers itself, choice—the hardest thing—becomes pliant. The moment fills with chance, the possibles not subservient to a will's law. Fulfilled thus, the present may further no human end but is of good fortune since it breathes with a circulation of air. In any event, time present reveals fruits not known to deliberative thought. Hope—when night comes to calculation—is one.

Wind, earth's breath, blows from hither to yon, from low down or high up, and is never without direction. In fact, where the wind blows defines the compass, as the compass measures the circle. Wind from the west comes with fair weather; from the east, with foul; from the north, with cold; from the south, with planting. Because of wind, the circumference does not spread uniformly round about a single point but varies in clemency, favor, rigor, and temper. Not every way toward which we head contains the same welcome. With wind comes weather (the word *weather* comes from the Old Slavic *vetra*) that follows the former's direction like a tail the dog. The wind that wakens us, while of chance, is never neutral, out of nowhere, or without special atmospheric effects. Wind brings that great metaphor of our mutable condition—the day's blue sky or clouds.

Weather invokes a terrestrial community. Being merely subject to weather, prone to its sea changes, we are anchored to earth. How does a human then differ from a rock, a tree, a deer, or any other living thing? Our humanity enjoys a wider communion than an earthly ecology. When we greet the harbinger of weather—wind—with respect, wind reveals itself as a dynamism, an everyday spirit able to carry us aloft toward heaven to fulfill our destiny as beings of the intermediate world.

With weather comes approval, disapproval, or indifference—an inner climate. *Hot* or *cold, wet* or *dry, stormy, clear,* or *cloudy*—these are terms of passion as well as meteorology. The synchrony of human mood and the day's weather is, unlike wind itself, not due to chance. Winds of anger, oppression, and despair—like the *fuhn*, sirocco, and Durango—best illustrate this fact. Moodiness and weather correspond because weather is the wind's emotion. "The wind in the *wu-t'ung* startles the heart, a lusty man despairs" (Li Ho, "Autumn Comes"). Like chance, the wind surprises our reactivity, husking its shell of indifference to expose a passionflower within.

The exquisite blossom houses intertwined serpents. One conceals, while one reveals, the human condition. Like wind and weather, feeling may captivate the attention with its violent, seductive, alluring character. Then inner state matches outer as closely as a westerly the wind sock. One succumbs to change rather than profits by it. Or captivity may alert a hidden eye of awareness to passion's guile. Then feeling's charm is momentarily broken to allow another reality to show itself. A depth in the whole self abounds with its secret alliance with Self.

In great times, the wind of change becomes almost legible—or feeling, transparent. Each seems to bear a signature of what is brewing. To divine change through wind or feeling is to know how presently to be.

Clouds scud, pennants fly, a mobile twirls, dust scurries away, smoke spirals skyward, reeds bend, and the waterfall sprays the left bank. Having direction, be it fickle or steady, wind flaunts it. Though it belongs to the invisible, wind is happy to point the way. Contrails of jets or high cirrus clouds advertise this truth while beyond the terrestrial atmosphere; in the sun's, the solar wind drives matter as small as electrons toward visibility. Catching wind of something, we know its whereabouts. By the same token, though inaudible, wind leaves sound tracks wherever it goes. Listen as it comes whispering over fields, whipping the grasses, snapping clothes on the line, and roaring uphill past your ears. It makes no secret of its comings and goings. Direction is a knack of wind. At dead calm, a sailor prays for it. A saint also, on dark, windless nights of the soul. Stagnant air would be more feared if ambitions of self-will were not mistaken for wind in our sails. The winds aloft differ from what drives us—as softness does from hardness—but only insight knows whether they should be in our face or at our back.

Does wind have a home?

The riddle has been put to many persons. Some say wind is a vagabond that scours earth in search of its home. Having none, it carries what it can and drops it when it stops to relate news of whence it has come. Others say it never had a place of its own but like a hermit crab scurries across the ground in search of another's. It has grown almost transparent, because it always has to hide. Still others argue that wind has a dwelling place and that, once rushing out, it—like the breath—never leaves. In ancient stories, Aeolus is keeper of the place. Neither mortal nor immortal, he plunges his sword into one side or the other of a cavern, from which direction wind issues. When he withdraws the sword, wind ceases. Odysseus received (from Circe) a sack of Aeolus's winds. They filled the sail of his ship without ever leaving their place.

According to other accounts, winds are souls of the dead. Wind's restlessness is a wandering soul in search of a resting place. Does not the soul escape a body at death with a sigh like the wind? In storm, at sea, or through the willow, lore hears the wind cry with the human voice of dead souls. On passing through the gates of hell, Dante's first perception is the same. He hears cries of suffering souls grate "as if a whirlwind sucked at sand" (*Inferno* 3.29). Their homelessness reflects a need for atonement. The wind too is beside itself, ecstatic or mournful, desirous of prayer, practitioner of magic, impetuous, and never abiding in one place for long. It quickens a hunger for life the way suffering of the now dead does.

There is another riddle: Why does wind blow the way it does?

The question asks after direction, and direction is what the question seeks. Wind, as I said, is an annunciation of direction. Direction belongs to chance and is heaven-sent. It necessarily unveils a route from source to outlet. Creatures able to heed and follow the wind's direction—eagles, hawks, and condors—are among the mightiest. A navigator knows wind arrives from up above. For him, wind moves from high to low pressure, to fill a trough, as it were, from the top. To trace the wind back to its lair is to meet a more intense energy. Like the breath, wind expends itself in blowing, and dies. When withdrawn into itself, wind is both most still and most threatening—the calm before the storm. Even if brutal or lashing, magnificent in its fury, it reveals a higher order of things—not in the "hand of God" but in earth's compass. And not only earth's; north-northeast, southwest, and due west are points that also set direction for the celestial sphere.

Since direction secretly conveys a locus of origin, even the lightest breeze can reveal an everyday order of things and, behind it, an inner order. The breeze can be our own, our respiration. Origin, destination, origin, destination: This is a mouse's roar of wind. The blowing wind makes its appeal to our senses: Purge yourselves of that which blocks an unadorned smell, touch, sight, taste, or sound of me. Then you will see direction that sights itself along a line toward a dim background of perception. The way passes between choice's constricted focus and the formless vision of the Self. They are Scylla and Charybdis, the one dashing our wits against a rock-hard surface, the other sucking us down to unfathomable depths. Who can pass between? Only that incomparable navigator, the audacious spirit of wind. Odysseus must make it his ally.

To traverse the Clashing Rocks needs good timing. One must take a chance and throw caution to the wind. How to do this with intelligence? Wind gives directions. Go out on any fine day, and try to catch the wind in your fist. Nothing. Now let go, and allow the wind to play against your open palm. Sensation awakens poise. Like a cat, you are ready to spring upon a first hint of the moment. No sign escapes your eye. No habit of impatience dulls instinct. When the rocks momentarily part and direction appears, nothing holds you back. Thus does wind steer a course that relates self to Self.

28

THE TOAST

It is feast time. An uninvited guest is riotously drunk. He wheels about the hall, invoking chaos and strewing good cheer along the way to a deep, dreamless sleep. He invokes the dream and all of grape's personae of myth. A fresh wine bowl stands unguarded. The guest carelessly fills an empty cup and is about to imbibe.

> But here Eryximachus broke in. Is this the way to do things, Alcibiades? he asked. Is there to be no grace before we drink? Are we to pour the wine down our throats like a lot of thirsty savages? (*Symposium* 214b)

Eryximachus the physician calls for a short pause before the onrush of appetite. Droning snores are bound soon to replace gales of laughter. The tide cannot be turned and anyway must not be scorned. What is his prescription? To allow a moment to lift glasses on high, to hold up their fullness so that heaven too may partake of the fruit of earth. The grace—a sigh—is to let thought enter, for thought then exclaims the virtues of existence for both worlds to hear. To life! the toast cries out. To life as it is lived!

According to some traditions, angels read the book of knowledge to an unborn infant while preparing it for terrestrial life. Its understanding grows full unto term, even throughout its journey down the birth canal. As the newborn struggles for a first breath, the angel of silence puts one finger to its upper lip, and the infant forgets. Each of us to the end of our days bears an indentation from the touch. It recalls our blessing and our task—of forgetting and remembering.

While we drink, a cup's rim barely grazes this small valley. A moment before, we raise it on high to invoke the spirit of the toast. To that being who affirms the *more* of life, our words fly. Cup brushes past lip as might an angel's wing. And we remember.

To toast is to invite knowledge to the banquet. Can bacchanal, dissipative or uproarious, come to a momentary stop? The one drunk or intent on becoming drunk must separate life from Life, a life that clings savagely to things from that graced by presence. This leave-taking is really the first after quitting the angelic realm. It is thus our first earthly one. It completes a cycle, being a return from the prenatal exodus. The toast remembers the angel of silence's act of erasure. The toast is a gesture of recognition. It loosens the cloak of false identity under which one has been living. The toast seals the departure with the goodwill of a traveler's community. It gives hope for the return.

The toast meets a physician's prescription for avoiding savagery. There are other ways of pausing over wine, namely, a libation and a blessing. The first pours out a portion to earth, while the second asks pardon for our need to imbibe. Only the toast celebrates human life, its contradiction and duality. It is neither penitent nor obsequious. By solemn words or light, oratory or stammering tongue, pet formula or heart-wrought utterance, the toast boldly declares itself. Never reticent or mealymouthed, it is audacious. It dares to send us off from comforts of self-oblivion to rigors of self-remembrance. How else to remedy what silence's angel has wrought?

The toast publicly celebrates our human lot. One turns to other means for private observances. Prayer and poetry are two. The toast has a different valence. "To your health!" "A vôtre santé!" "L'hayem!" "To the good life!" The gesture unseals the lips of a whole assembly and bonds all in a communion of knowledge. It is intended for everyone, butcher and baker, soldier and thief, pauper and prince. The mood is festive, for only the feast provides tonic against a deadly paralysis of farewell. Without the fiesta, departure is a wrenching away, a subtraction or sacrifice. One or more are separated from those remaining, perhaps forever. Yet joy attends, because the toast remembers a pageant of life, both going out and coming back. In a raised cup is hope that to embrace a life within life will add to communal wealth. All who hear the utterance participate in its act of renewal.

Not all separations are attended by the spirit of the toast. For one who journeys forth without its joyful remembrance, no palliative is given for pain of leave-taking. Departure is a matter of despair and confusion. Love is no companion along this way. A break is possible only for an ascetic whose rigor of mind wills the undesired and desires only what is willed. Much must be endured; listen.

> And if, said I, someone should drag him thence by force up the ascent which is rough and steep, and not let him go before he had drawn him out into the light of the sun, do you not think that he would find it painful to be so haled along, and would chafe at it, and when he came out into the light, that his eyes would be filled with its beams so that he would not be able to see even one of the things that we call real? (*Republic* 515e)

When compulsion undertakes to journey, there is neither joyous homecoming nor community to absorb newly won knowledge into its heart. A pilgrim is solitude, and solitude keeps what it gains to itself. Because a return is unwelcome:

> Would he not provoke laughter, and would it not be said of him that he had returned from his journey aloft with his eyes ruined and that it was not worthwhile even to attempt the ascent? (*Republic* 517a)

So is a prize, if it be that. For without the toast's vital confirmation, what else vouchsafes a traveler's penetration of the middle world? On many a day, solitude travels under the cloak of fantasy.

Thus does this everyday spirit draw humans together. One moment, preoccupation weighs us down heavily. The next, we lift glasses—and ourselves from ordinary life—in order to get an angle on truth. Suddenly it is a celebration. Friend and enemy alike are involved. Having stepped out a bit from ourselves, we toast the journey and down the cup. And if the cup is poisoned? "Hamlet, this pearl is thine, here's to thy health," says Claudius, deceit on his tongue (*Hamlet* 5.ii). The utterance, however, has more force than his evil intent. It brushes conspiracy aside with a neat stroke and restores a memory that undoes the angel's amnesiac work. If the king toasts, then the spirit cannot be unsaid. After so much dilatory action, Hamlet is recalled to his almost-blunted purpose. This is the miracle of the toast. Claudius's plot misplays, and the prince gains his revenge, his knowledge, and his return.

For want of a good toast, we go dry. Even after drinking, dryness remains, for wine alone slakes no real desire—unless for dreamless sleep. There, waters of life buoy us up and replenish the wells. But can we be restored to life in the midst of life? That is a desire for reality; "fill me a bottle of sack, our soldiers shall march through," says Falstaff (*Henry IV, Part I*, 4.ii). So dammed up are the waters within, that chronic thirst goes unnoticed. What does the doctor prescribe? The toast that exclaims an awareness of inner drought. Its roots are in the Latin *torrere*, "to cause to become dry," and itself grows from the same parched soil. A *tostee* was originally a grilled slice of bread, dipped in wine to be drunk to another's health. The *tostee* took that which had been consumed by fire and by submersion replenished its waters. The toast embodies a similar act. It grips the thirst and dunks it in the life-giving flow until satisfied.

No draught quenches. He who bursts drunkenly in upon the assembly would drink more. Only the proposal of a toast gives him pause from savaging the wine bowl. It spurs an intelligence that speaks a love of life. For it is love that gathers a community in front of the one who separates from everyday ways. Love sweeps a dwelling place clean of animosity and prepares for the journey, just as love steadfastly awaits the homecoming. Of what does love speak? Our idiocy. Wisdom may protest with Socrates: "Do you want to make me look a fool with this eulogy, or what?" (*Symposium* 214e). But since idiocy is forgotten when we are touched by the angel of silence, such words bring us back to ourselves.

"To no more bruised bones!" A wind blew the ladder over, but no one was badly hurt. Forethought might have prevented an accident, but forethought was absent. Afterward, during the feast, one thinks well of the moronic tendency. In the fable, father and son tote their donkey on a pole in order not to abuse it with their weight. On a bridge, it kicks one and falls into the river to drown. "To ingenious solutions!" Chicken Little is hit by an acorn and deduces that the sky is falling. Others agree, and all become dinner for an opportunistic fox. "To brilliant deductions!" To harken to the levity of pretension is to toast idiocy. To toast idiocy is to make room for a new mind. "Give up ingenuity, renounce profit, and bandits and thieves will disappear." Toast after toast, one moves away from the ordinary along the way to the Self.

The toast celebrates drought's end and the cooling of an over-heated intellect. For no reason, reason takes umbrage at idiocy's coming to light. Here lies a misunderstanding. The word itself derives from an ancient Indo-European root *sued-*, meaning "separate." The Greek *idios* conveys a sense of being proper to oneself (thus apart from life's claims on oneself), and survives intact in the word *idiomatic*. To cut through accretions and come to essence is to uncover one's idiocy, a cause for celebration. Extraneous notions about self drop away, and health again flourishes. To the idiot, hale and hardy. *Santé*!

"Give from your bowl the wine of *they shall be given to drink of pure wine*, for only new joy will cut away anxiety" (Rumi). Thus, Rumi advises welcome of the toast's generous spirit. This everyday spirit hovers above the wine's surface, a conduit through which higher energies blend with those of the fermented grape. It quickens a body with remembrance and pleases heaven by its good grace. Among beings of the intermediate realm, the toast's longevity varies inversely with its shortness. A long-winded toast brings a company nothing but a restive forgetfulness.

A toast, moreover, never suffices unto itself. It invites the wine of purity, heaven's gift, in order to drink of earth's. If its few words fail to raise the cup's rim past the valley in the upper lip, they are hollow. Not to drink is ungrateful. Now the cup is lifted, now the toast is proposed, now the wine is drunk, now talk of love proceeds.

The End

Made in the USA
Lexington, KY
03 November 2015